# Me, My Selfies and I...

by

## Mark Pettifer

A humorous exploration
of me for my family and
friends

ISBN-13: 978-1497569805

ISBN-10: 149756980X

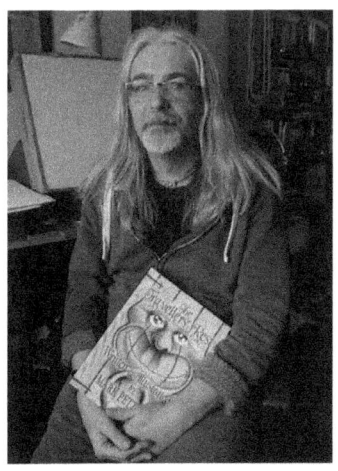

Photo taken by Sonya Homer

When I released my second book, Pipe Fairies Revolution, I was asked by one of the local newspapers to do a 'selfie' for an article they were writing on me. I don't have a digital camera other than the one on my phone and I just could not suss out how to take a picture with me well framed in it. In the end a friend took the snap and it was published.

I still haven't got the foggiest idea how to take a selfie on my phone and I still don't own a digital camera. What I do have, however, is the ability to draw and sketch. After seeing a few selfies my friends had posted on Facebook I drew myself and posted it. After a few encouraging comments and 'likes' I posted another. I then sketched a few more pictures of me and more heartening comments came as I documented my day. Very soon it got silly and I started to make characters out of my face.

Mark Pettifer...XX...

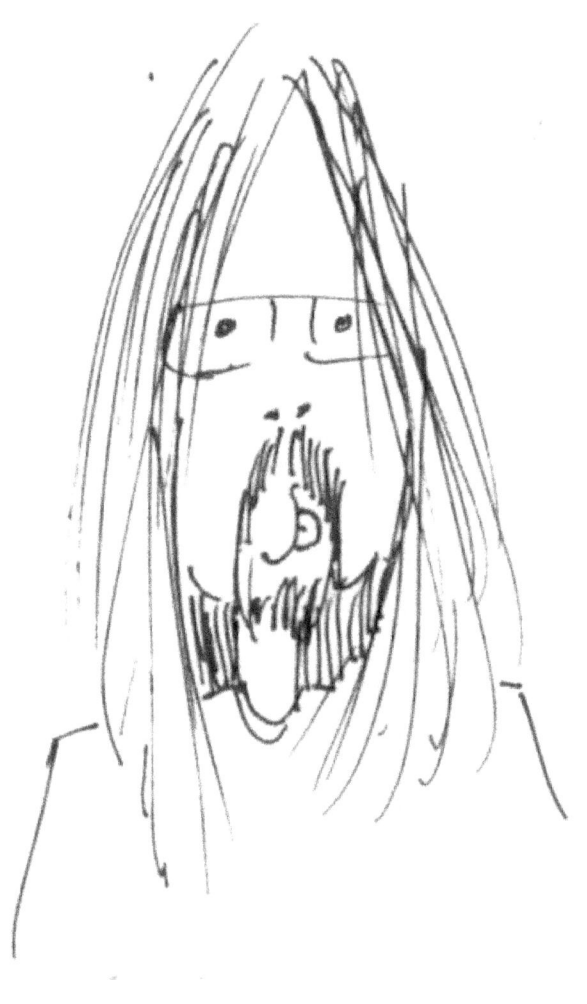

Me today...X....

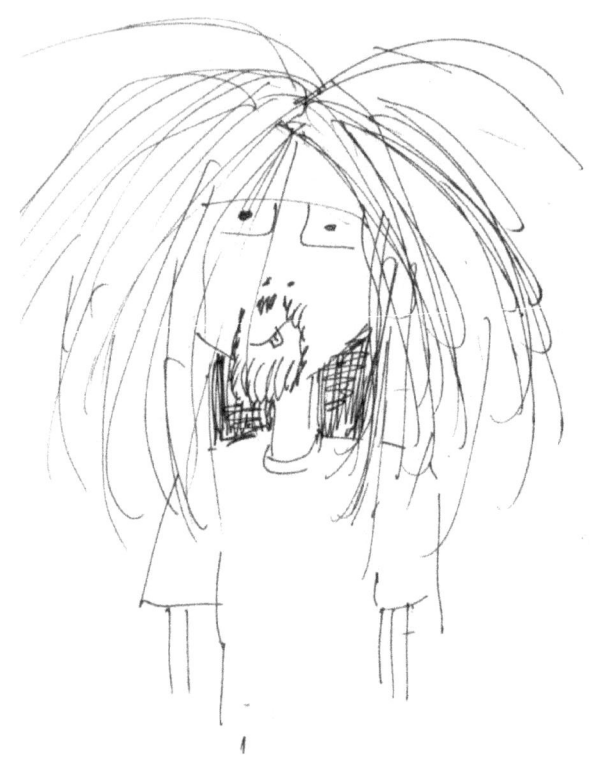

Just woke...X...

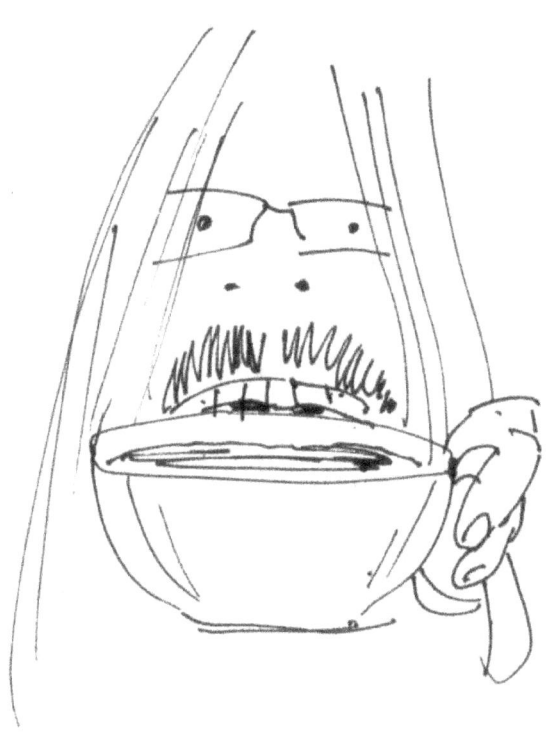

Slurping...X...

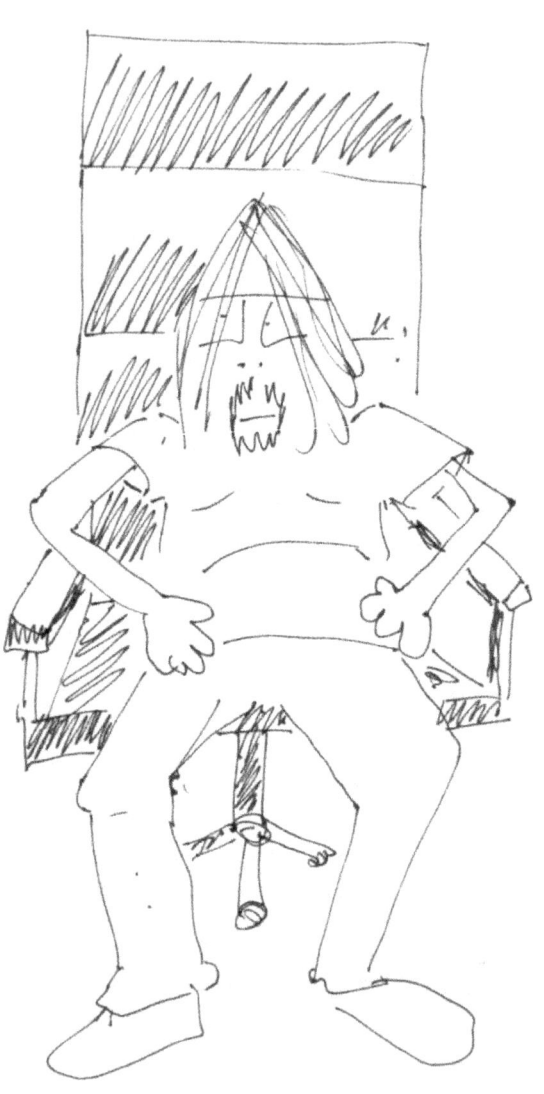

How tired am I?...X...

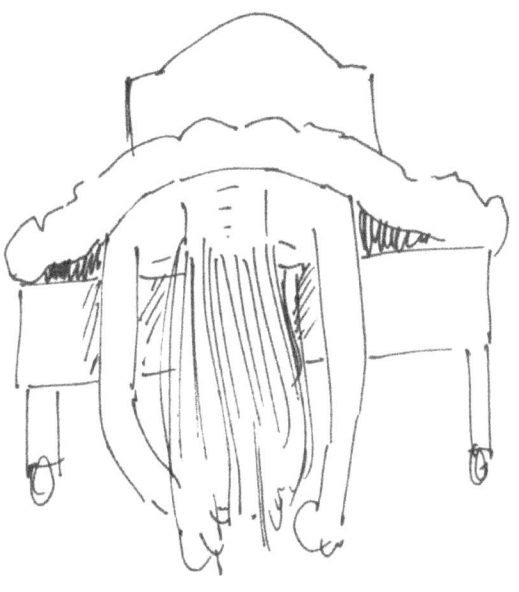

A fidgety night's sleep...X...

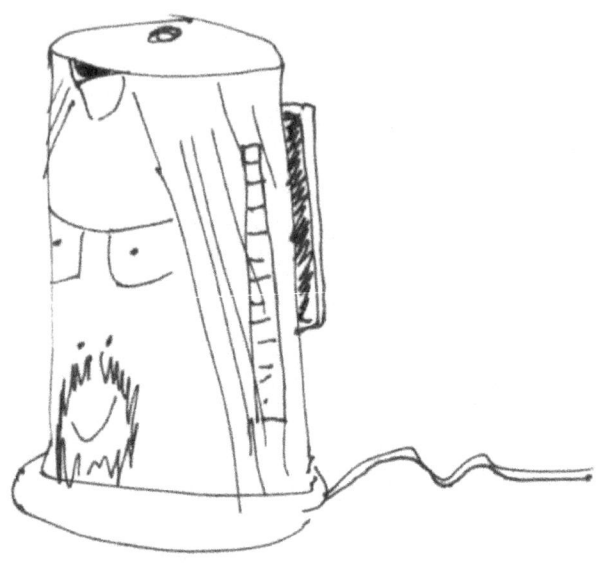

Mark the kettle... will someone please stop pressing my button?...X...

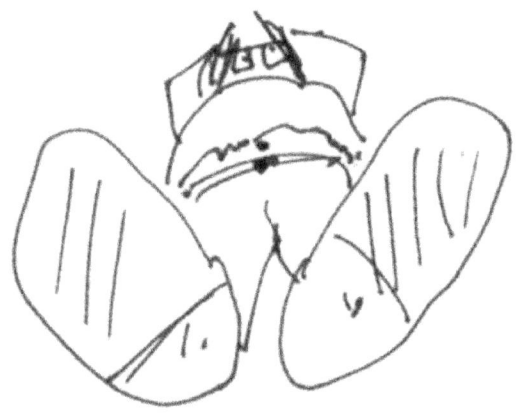

A rest after tea...X...

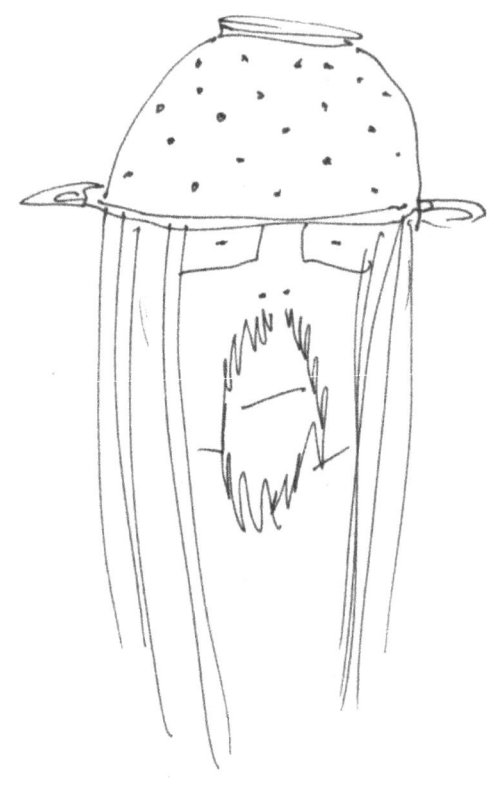

Are you sure it's only
sand in the air?...X...

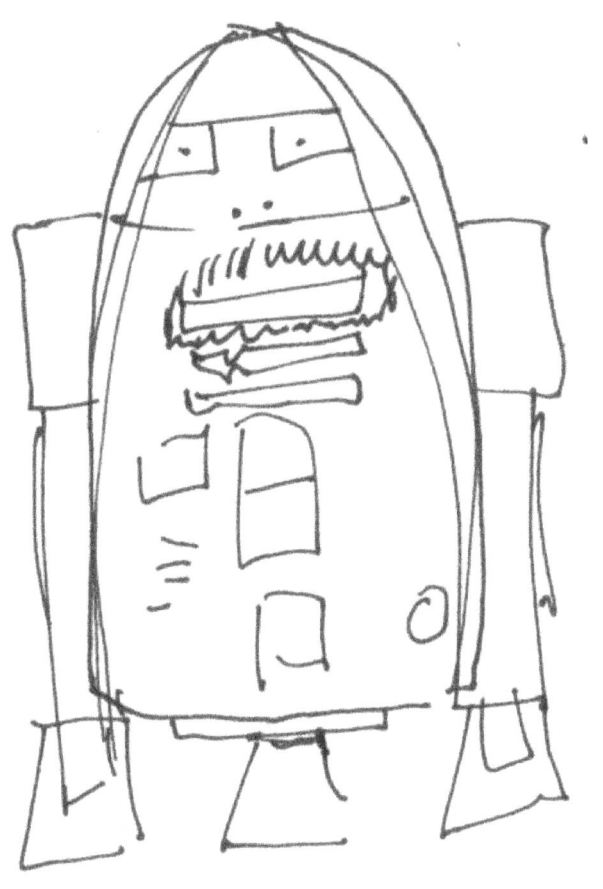

Mark2D2...X...

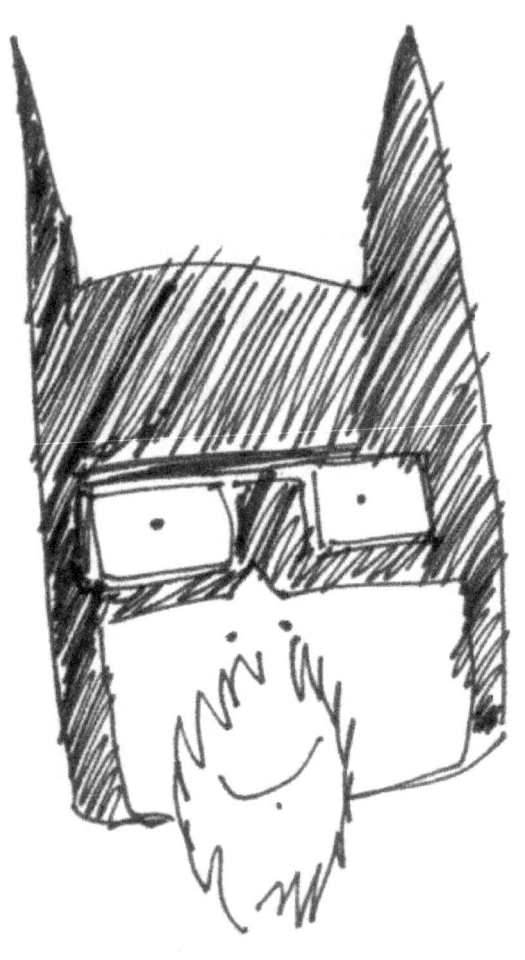

Batmark...X...

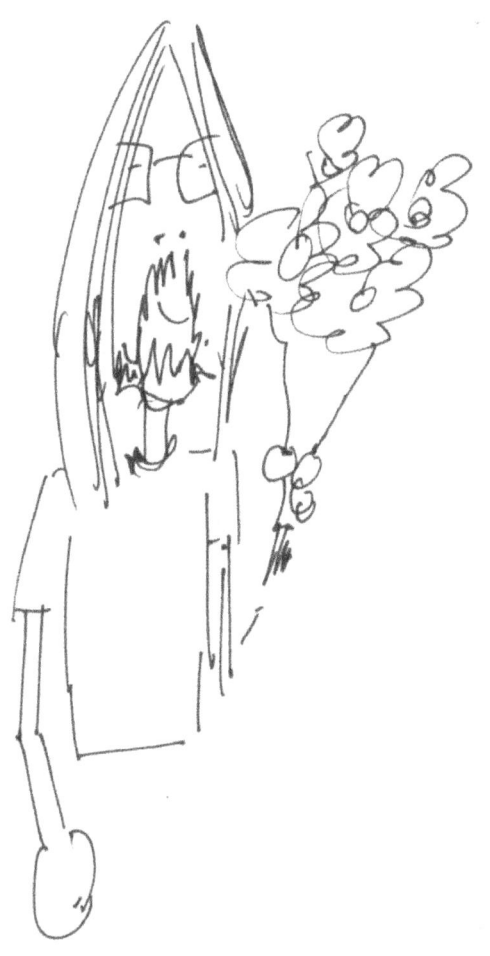

Because I love you...X...

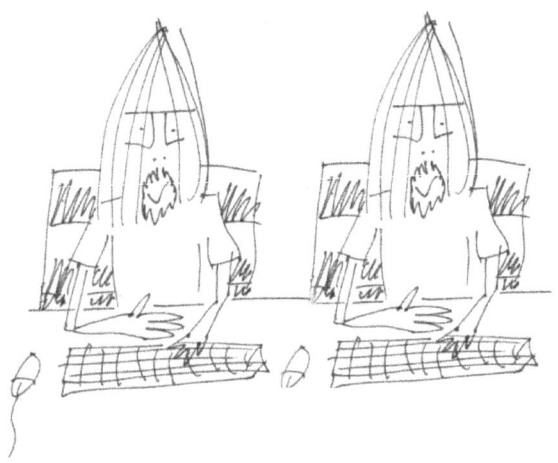

Before and after I get an
amazing publishing deal
– still pending...X...

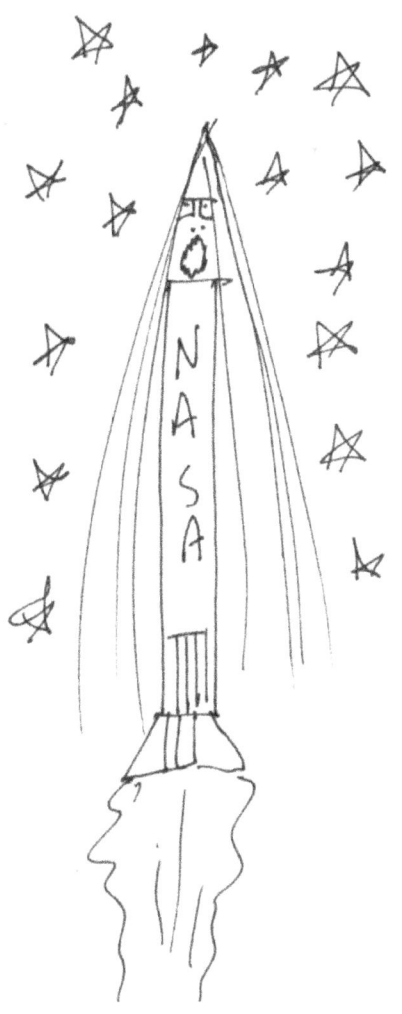

Blast off!...X...

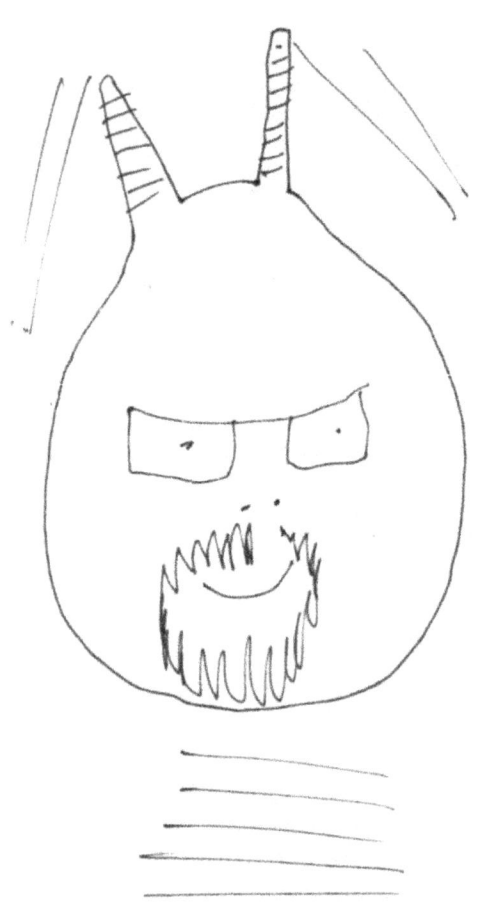

Boing!...X...

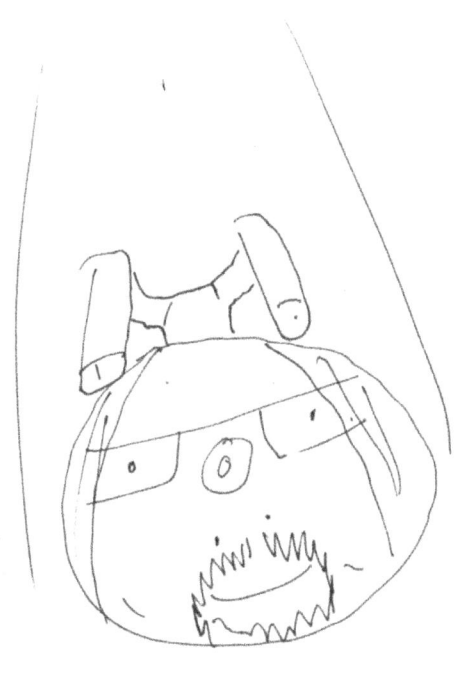

To boldly go...X...

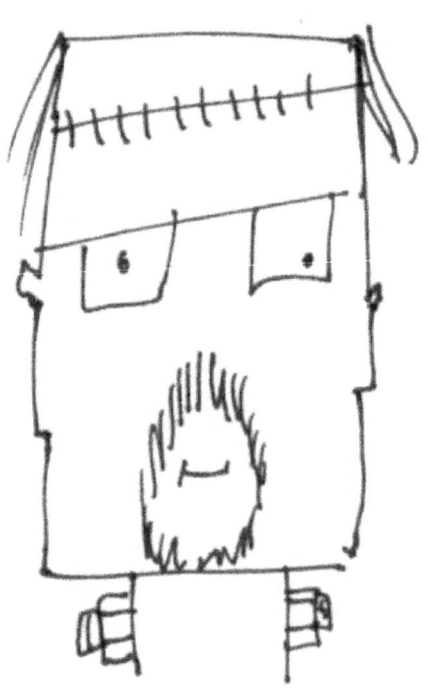

Nuts...X...

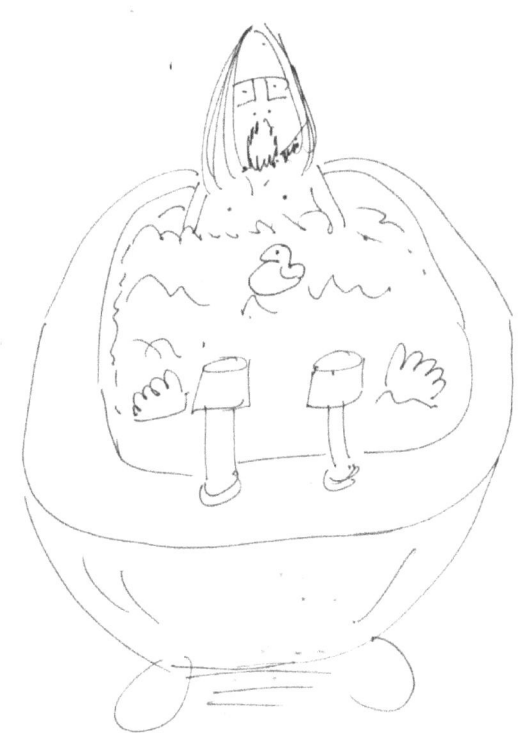

Bubble time...X...

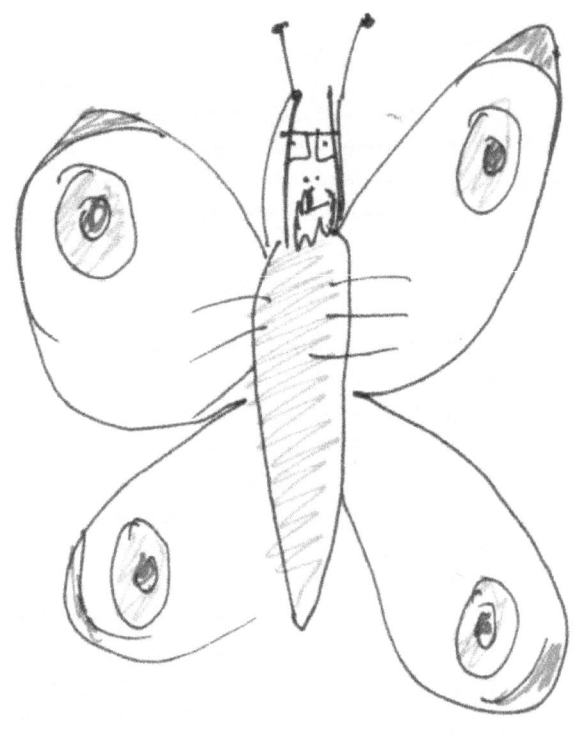

Mark the butterfly...X...

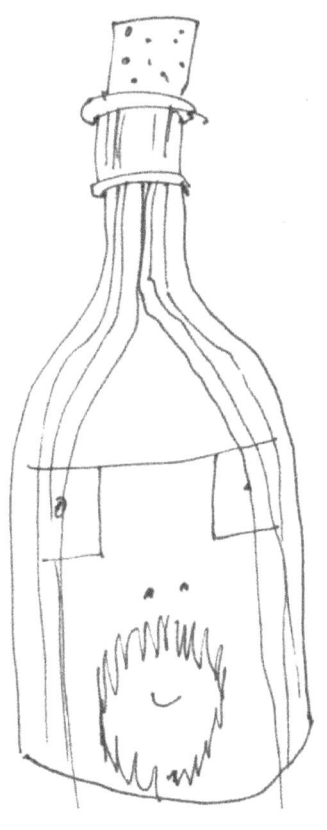

A good year...X...

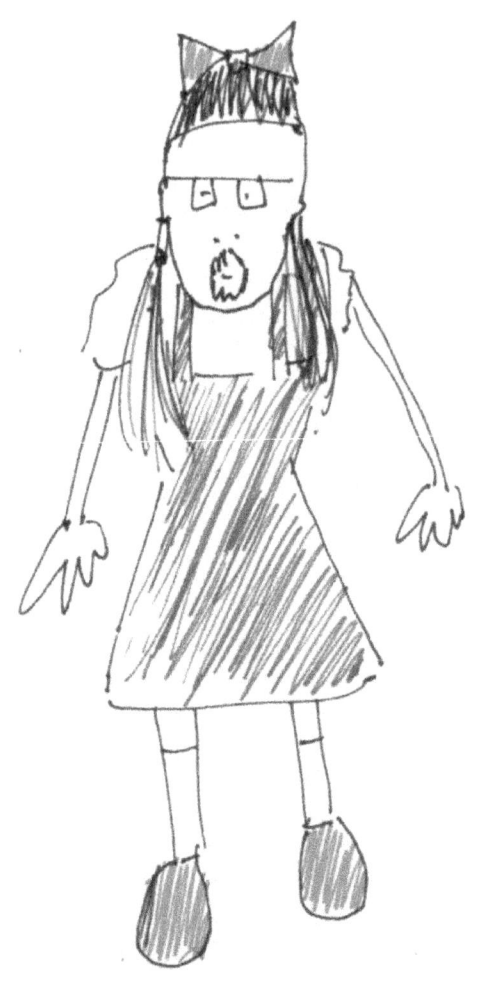

Click what together?...X...

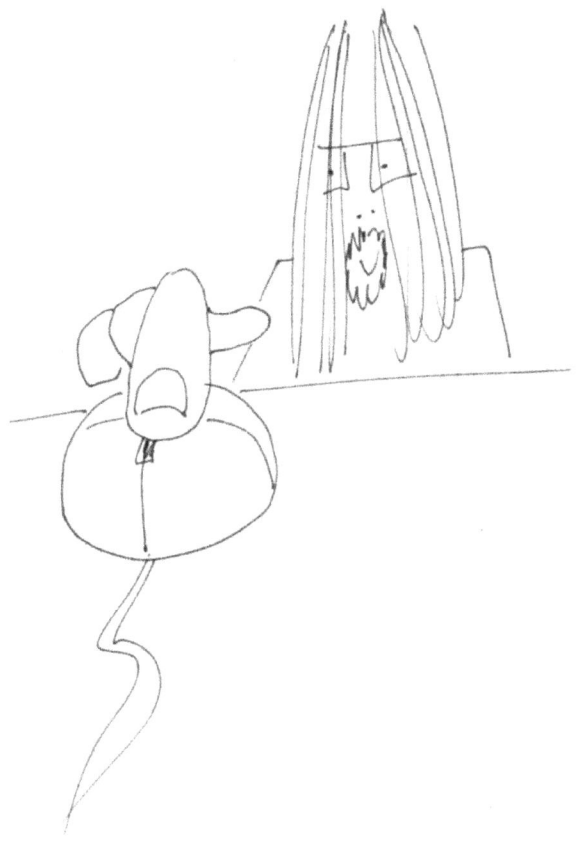

Clicking 'like' a lot...X...

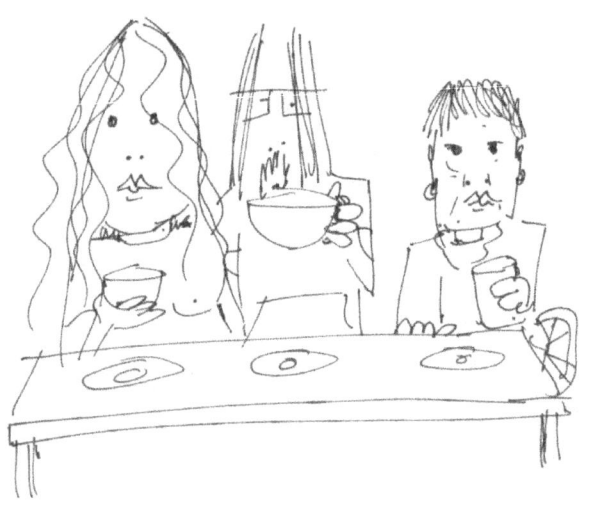

Coffee with friends...X..

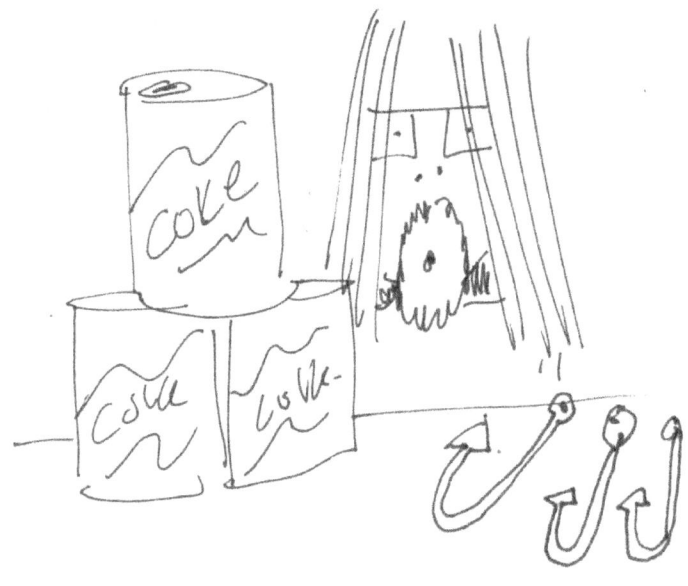

Coke and hookers...X...

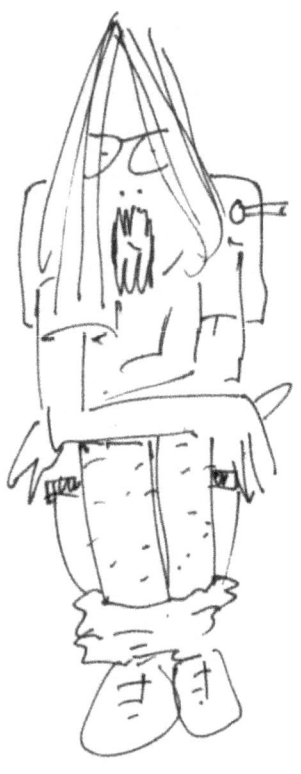

Contemplation...X...

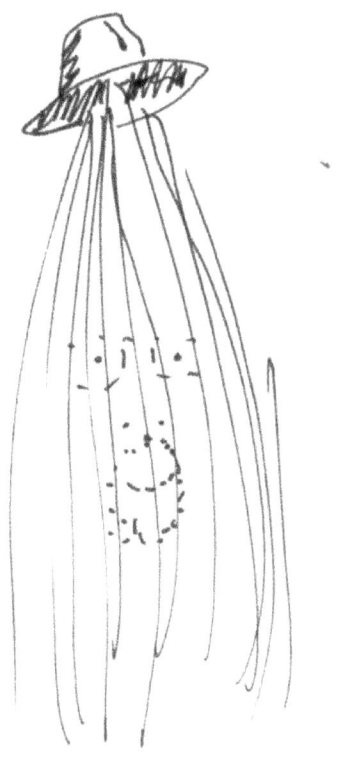

Cousin Itt...X...

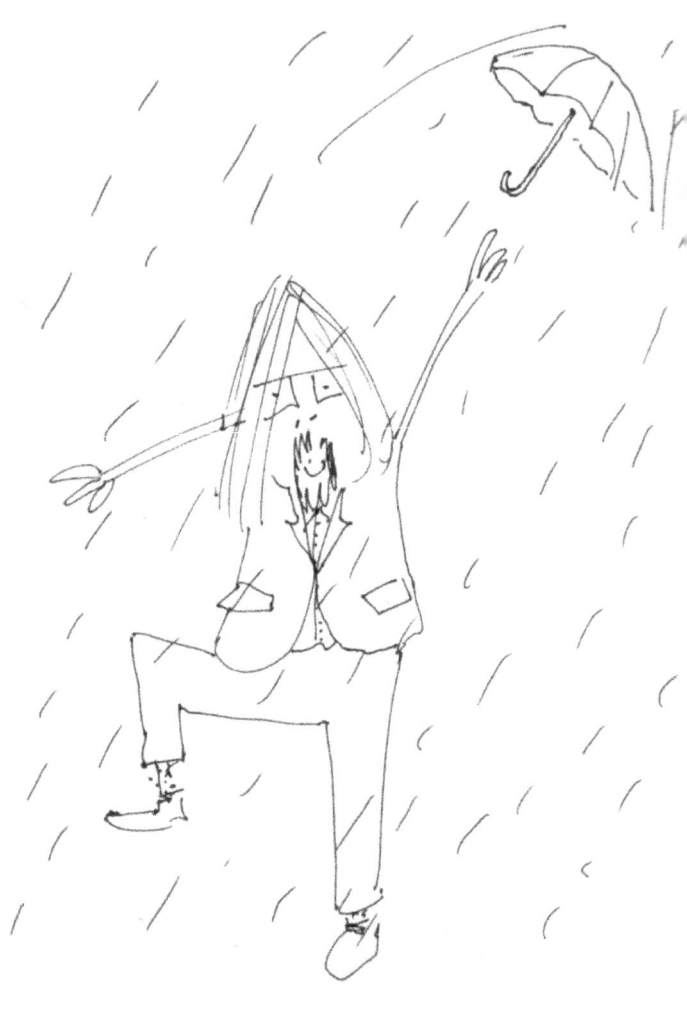

'Singing and dancing in the rain'...X...

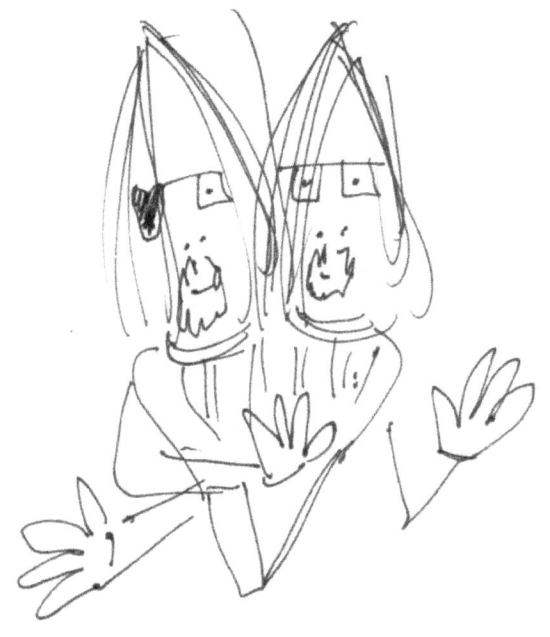

'Don't try and out weird
me, three eyes. I get
stranger things than you
free with my breakfast
cereal'...X...

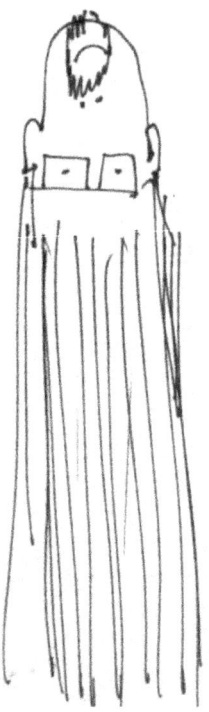

Down under...X...

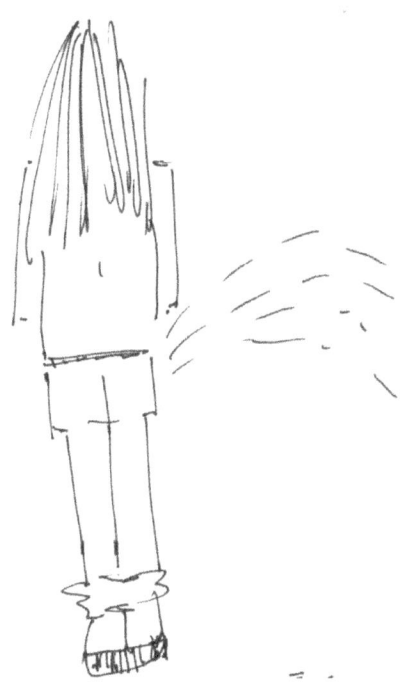

*Every fifteen minutes...X...*

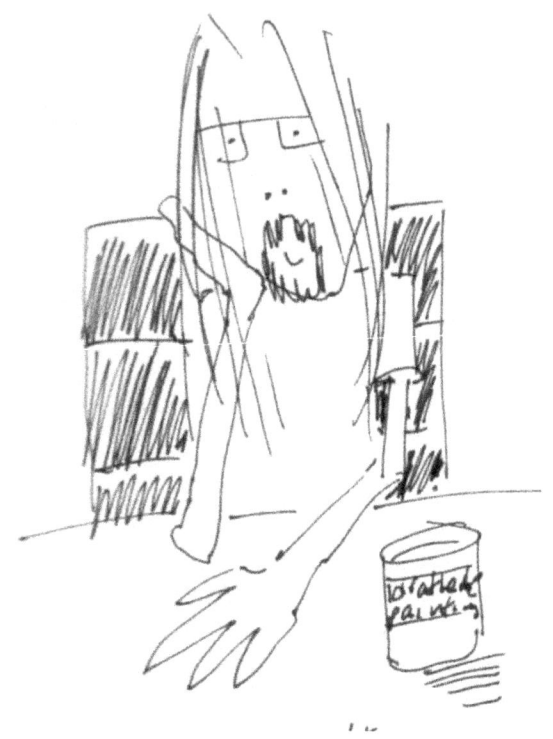

Exhausted after my
morning out...XX...

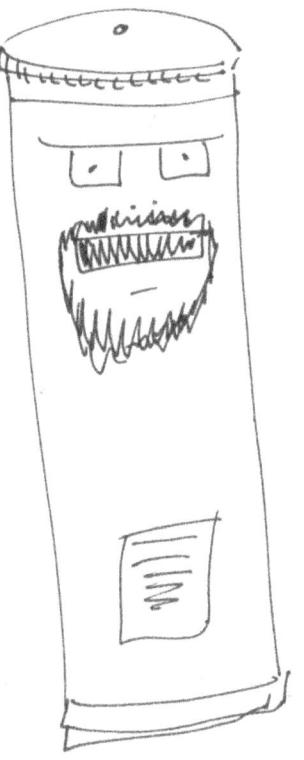

Ex-Royal Mail

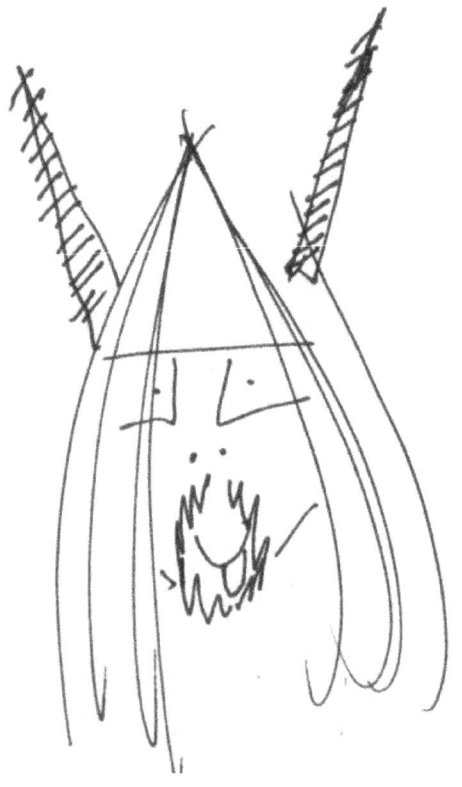

Feeling horny...X...

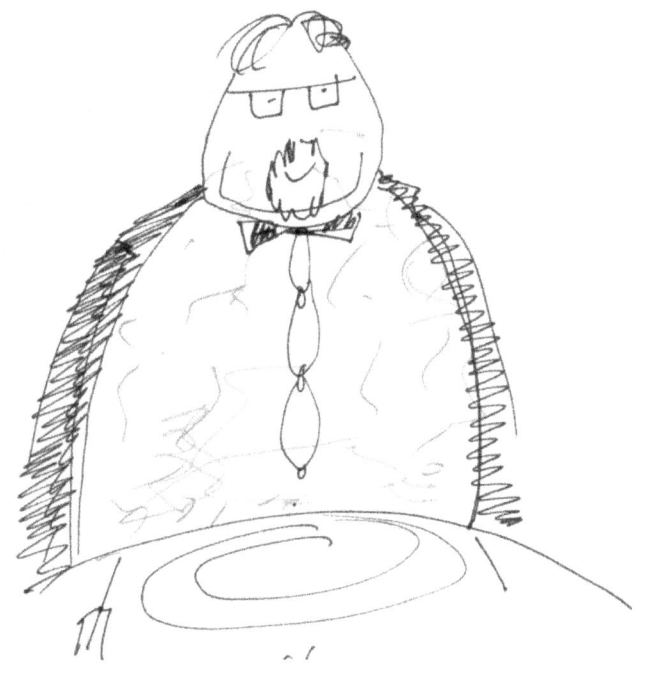

Fuck off...X...

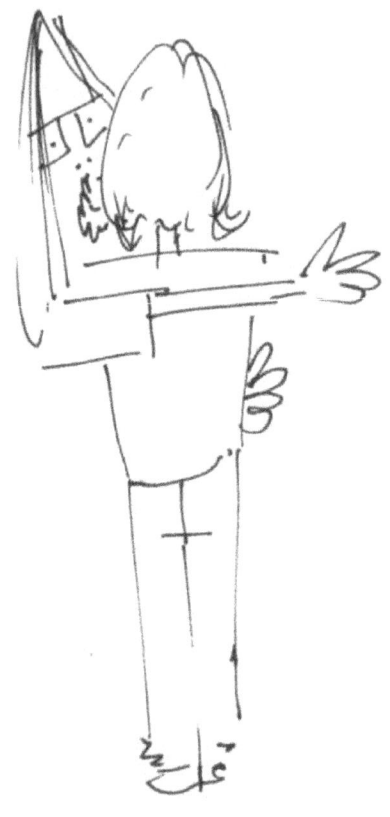

Giving my mum a peck
on the cheek...X...

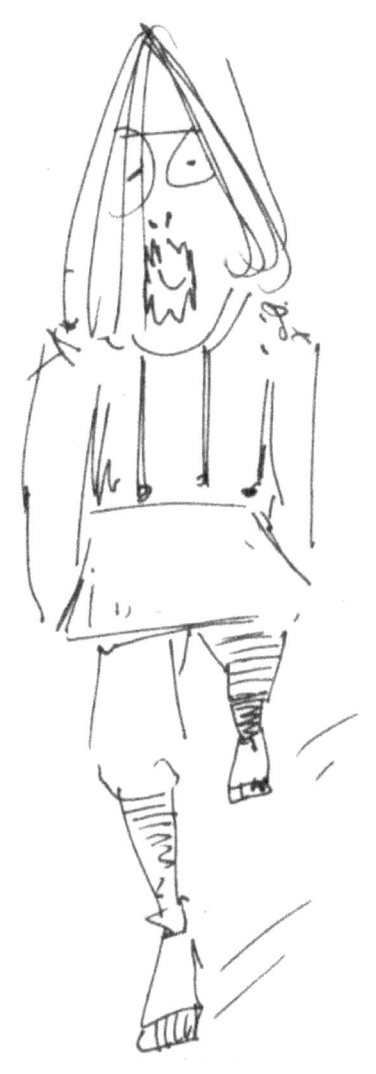

Off to meet with friends...X..

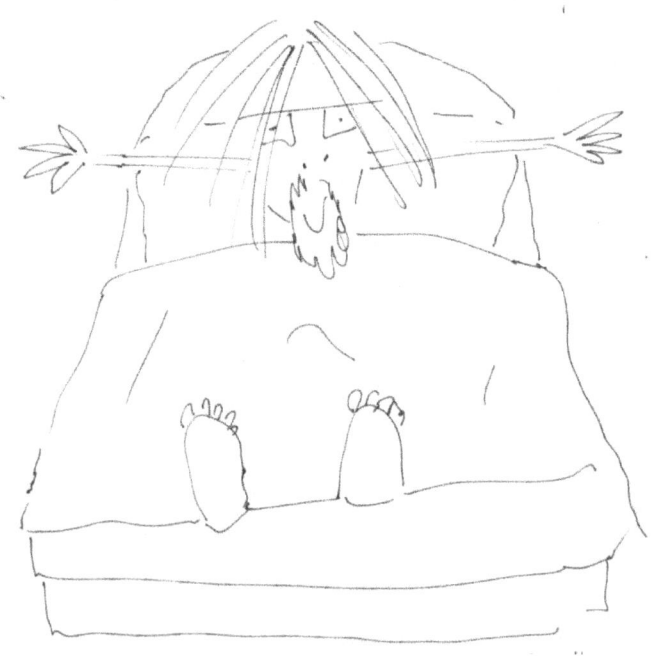

Good morning world and
other places...X...

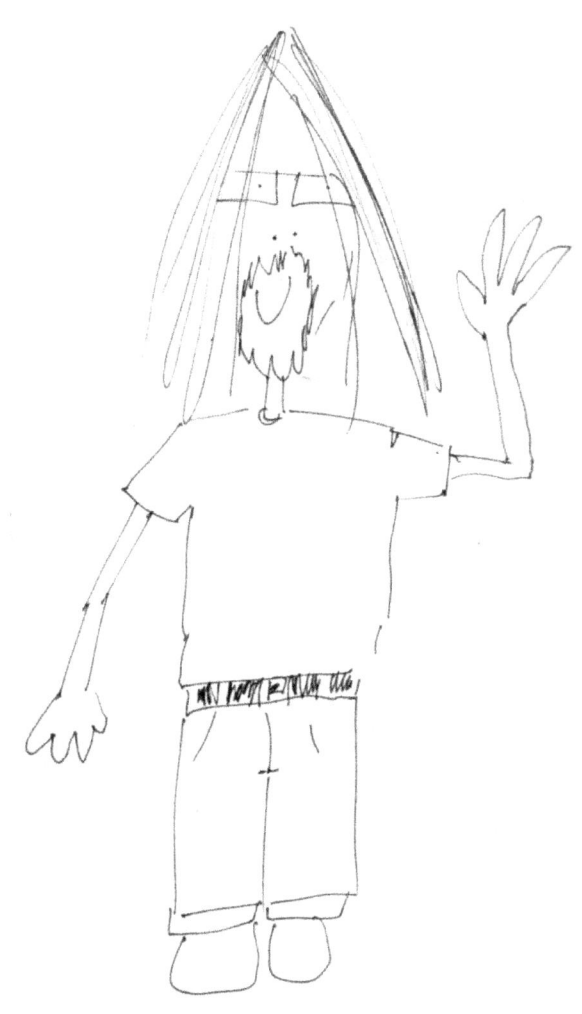

I'm up...X...

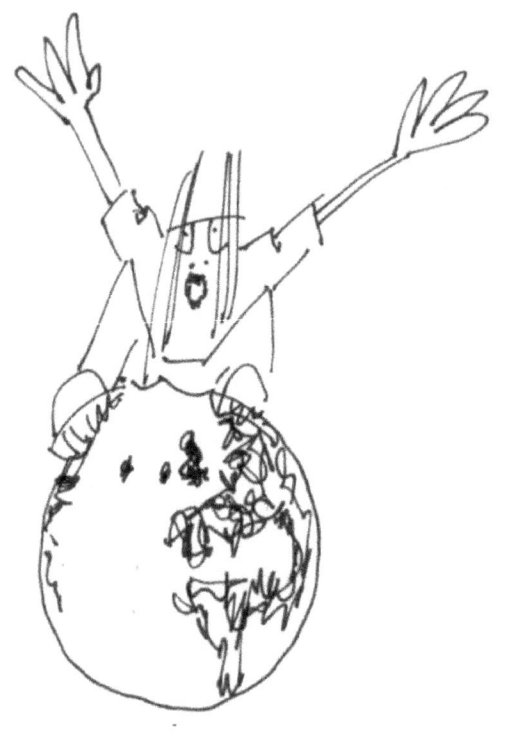

Hey, Mark, I'm on top of
the world...X...

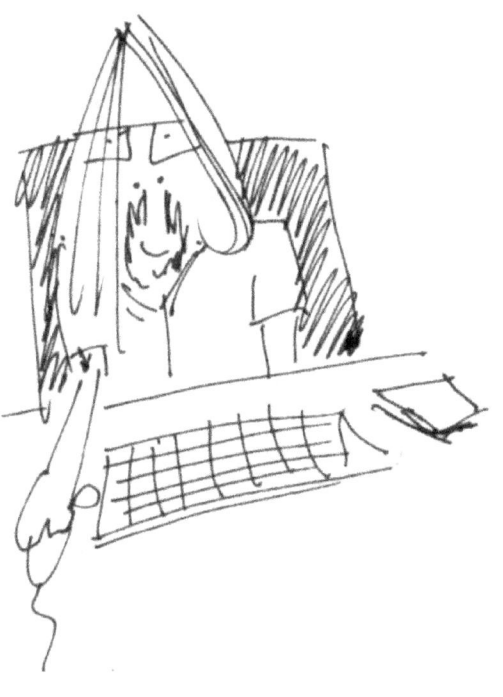

Home...X...

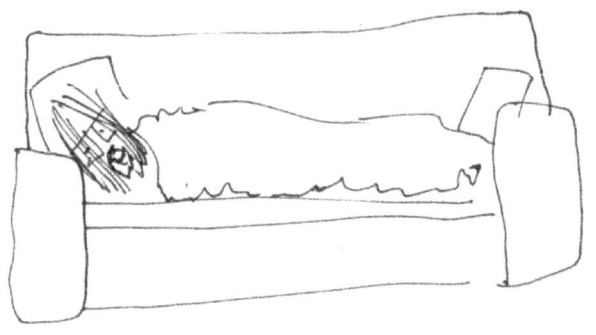

How I feel at 18:43 and
39 seconds...X...

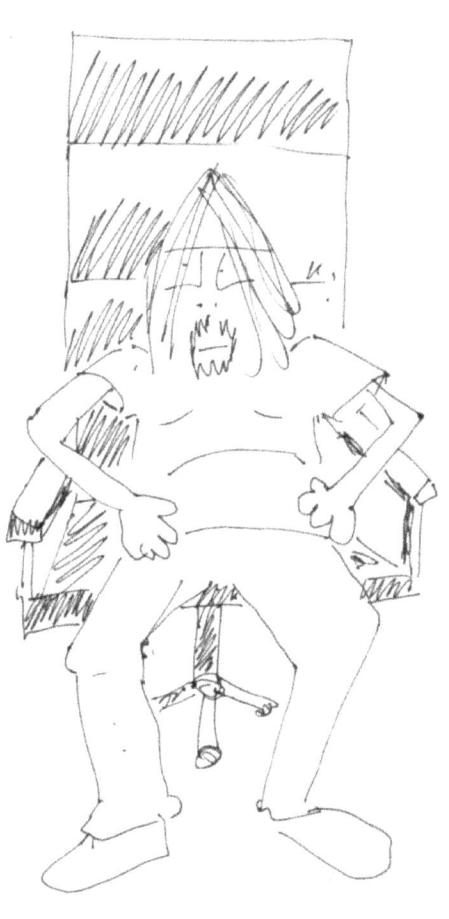

How tired am I
again?...X...

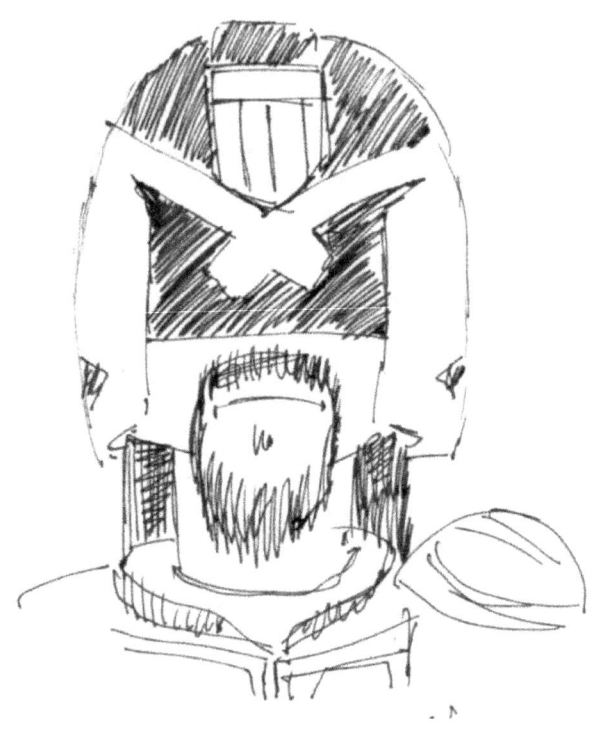

I am the LAW!...X...

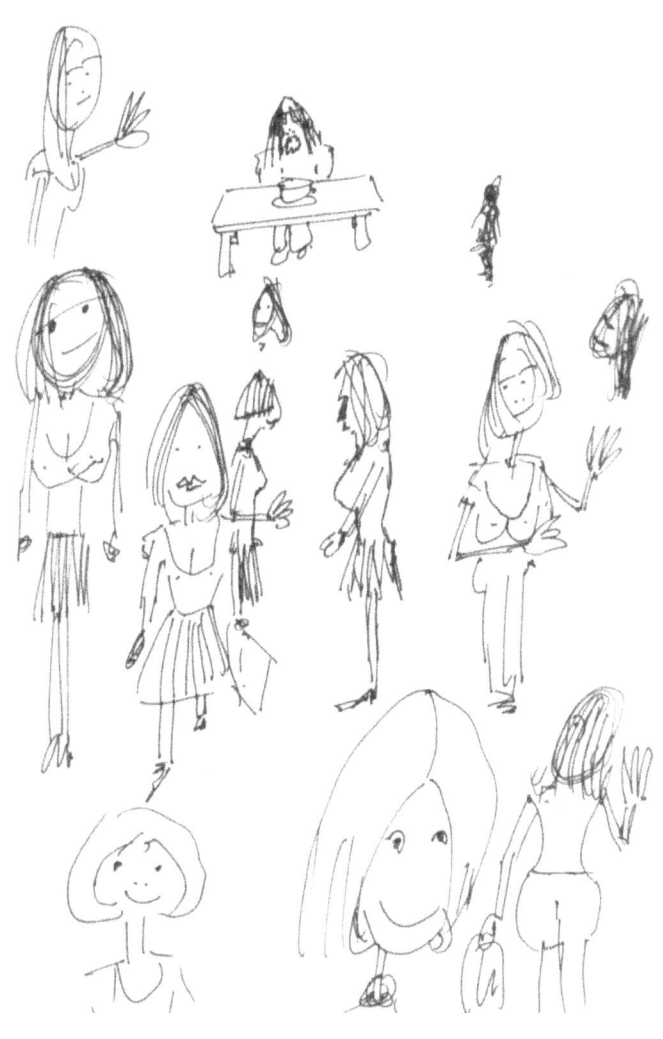

People watching... some might
call it letching...X...

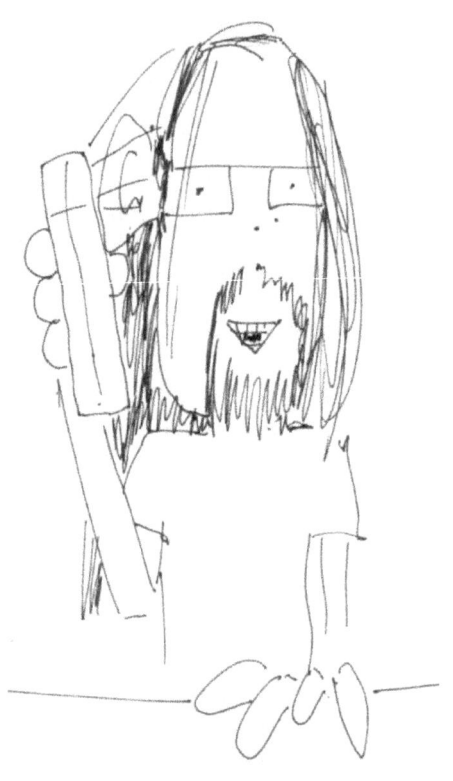

I had an unpleasant
phone call...X...

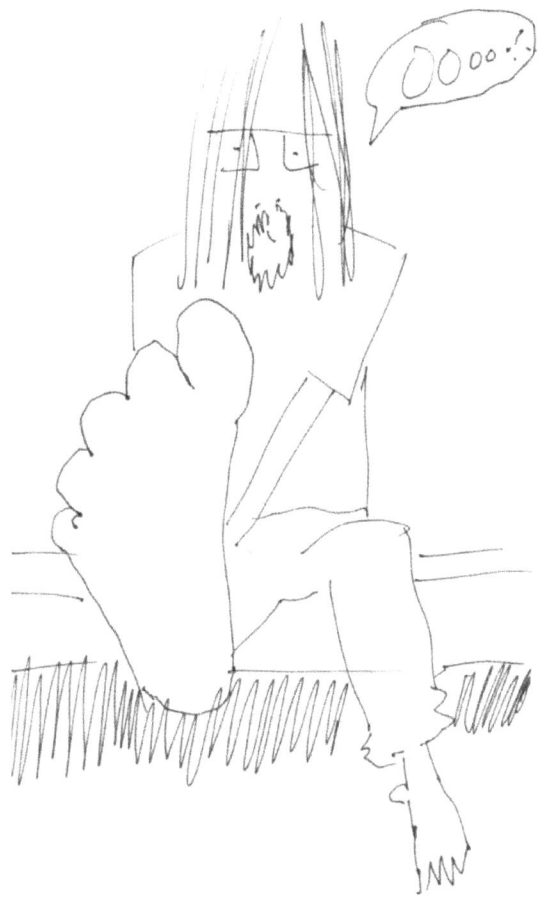

It hurts to put my socks
on today...X...

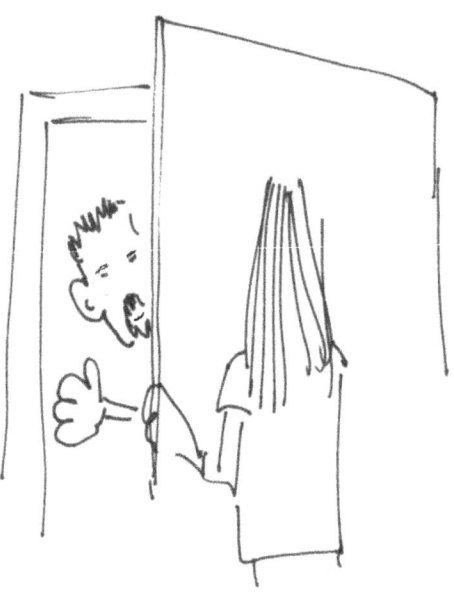

Here's Tom – pre-
empted...X....

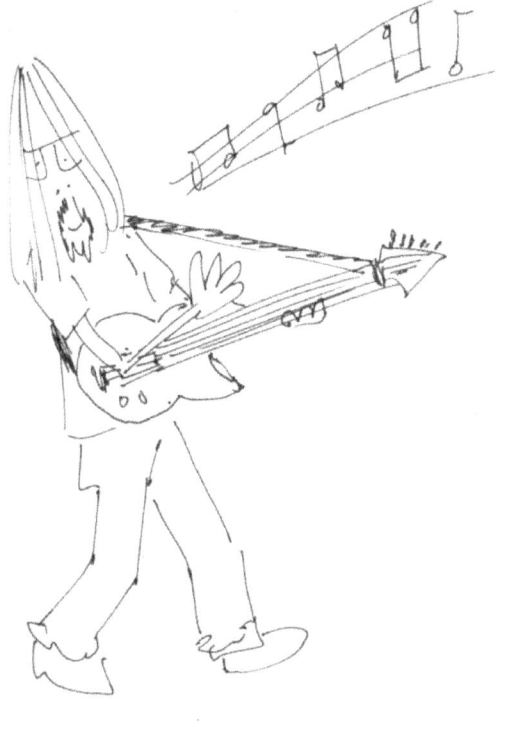

Join the Foo Fighters...X...

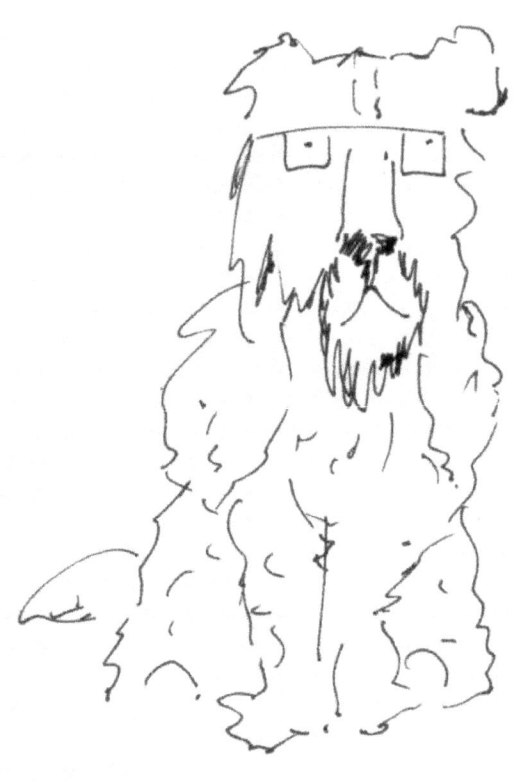

'Lassie come home!'

'Fuck off! It's too
dangerous there...X...

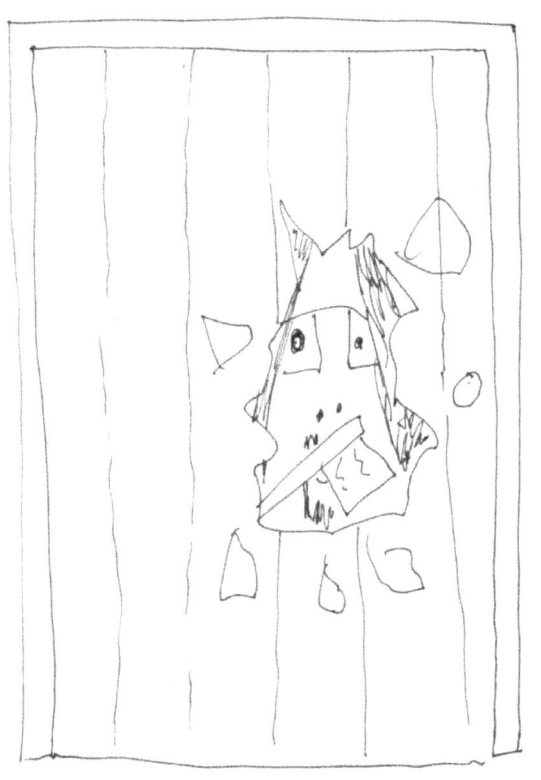

'Little pigs!'...X

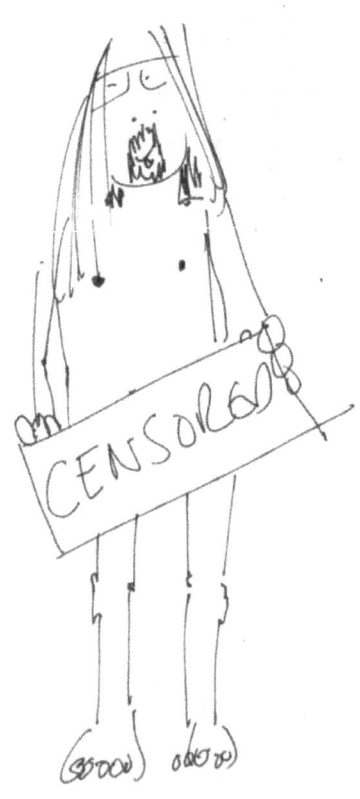

Looking for my
clothes...X..

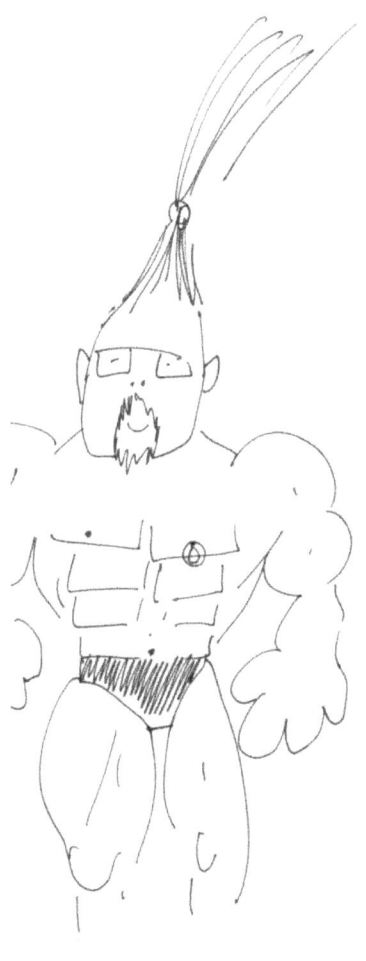

Lying...X...

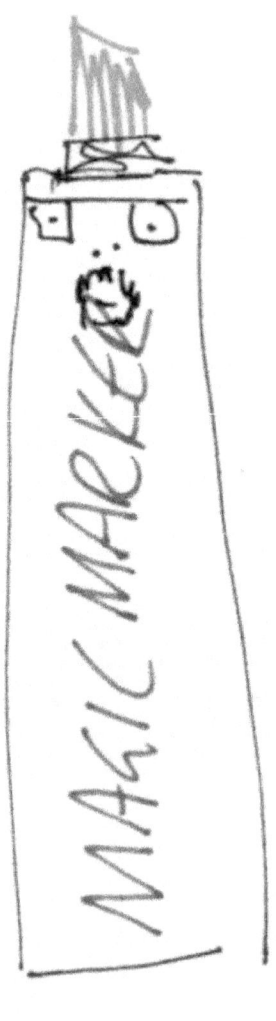

Magic Mark-er...X...

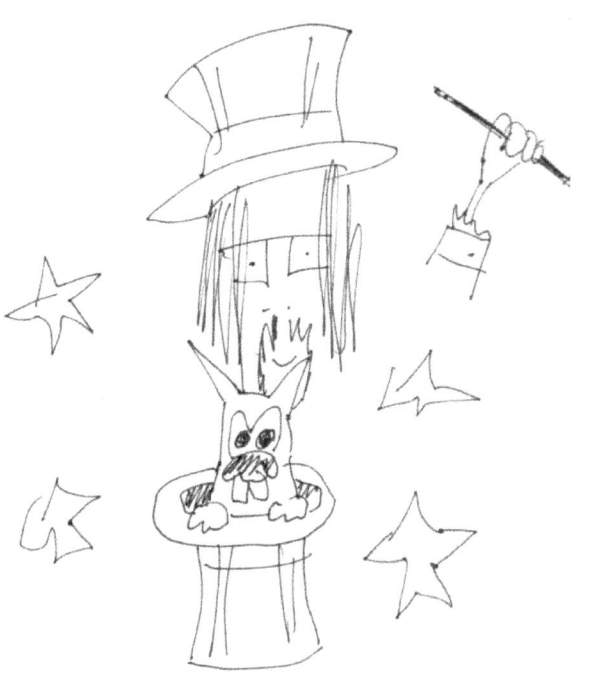

Magic!...X...

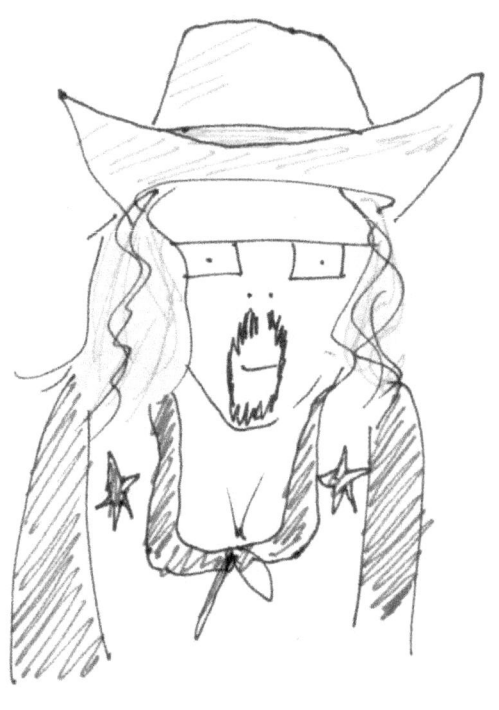

Mark does Dallas...XX...

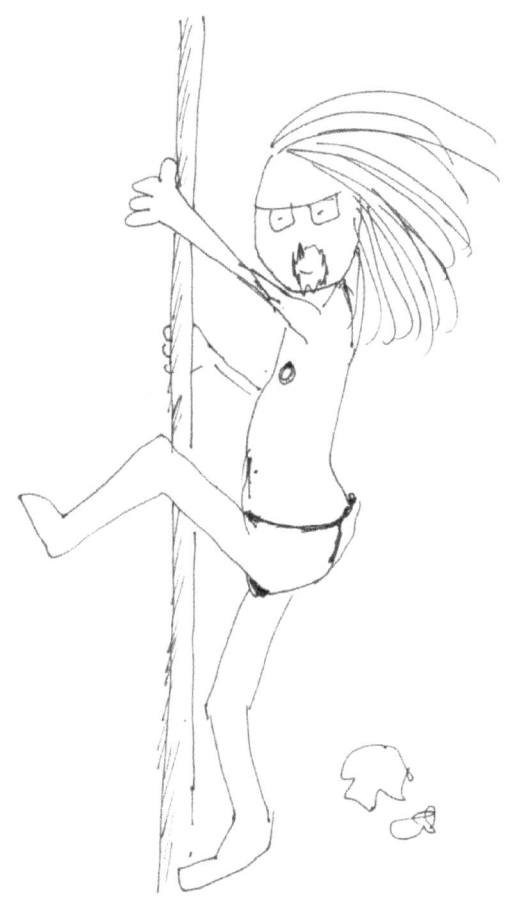

Drinks too much and
pole dances...X...

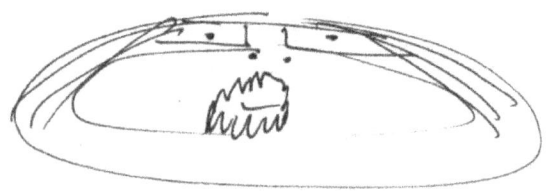

Mark the plate...X...

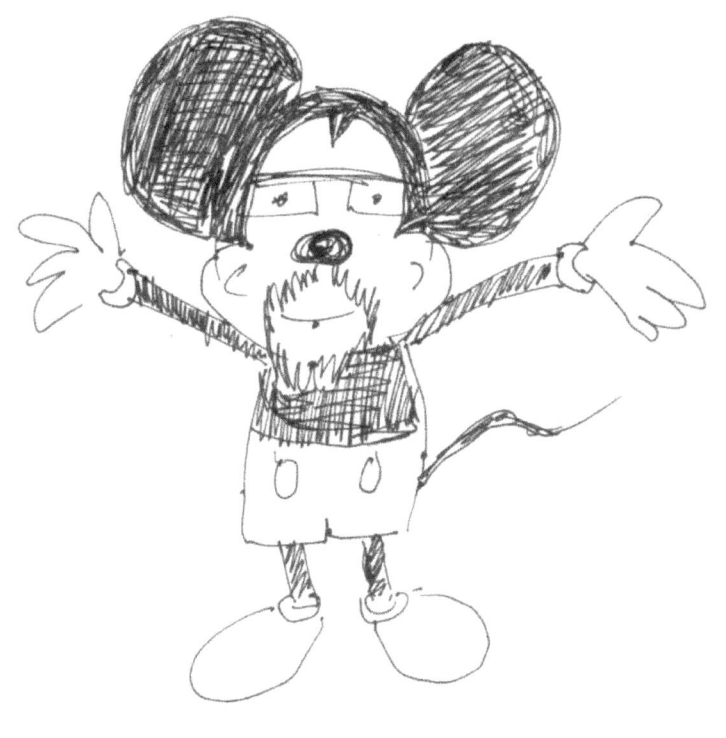

M-A-R-K-M-O-U-S-
E...X...

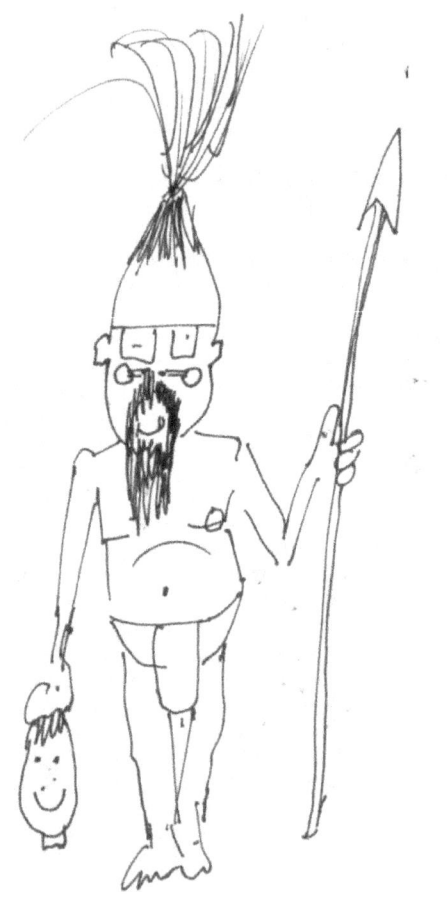

Mark of the wild...X...

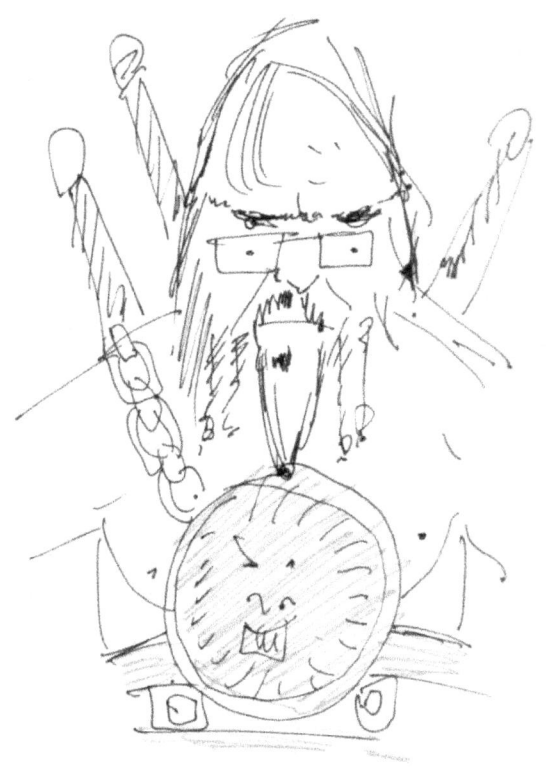

Mark the barbarian...X...

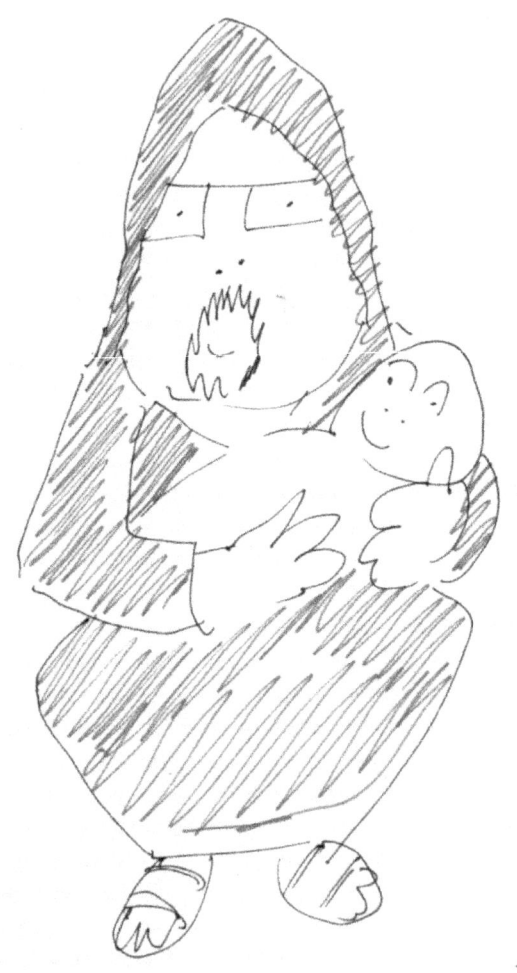

Mark-donna and child...X...

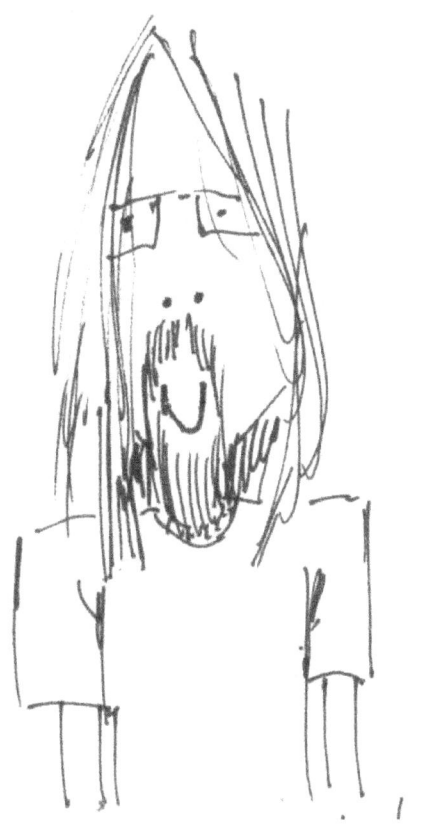

A little later on...X...

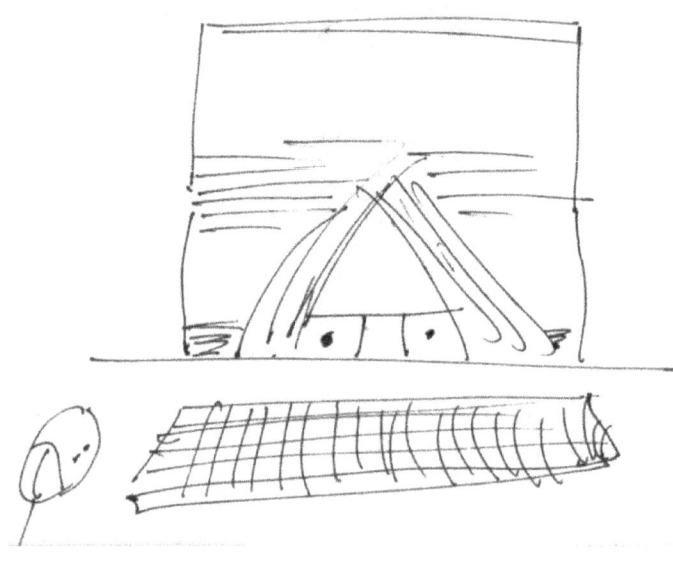

Fading fast...X...

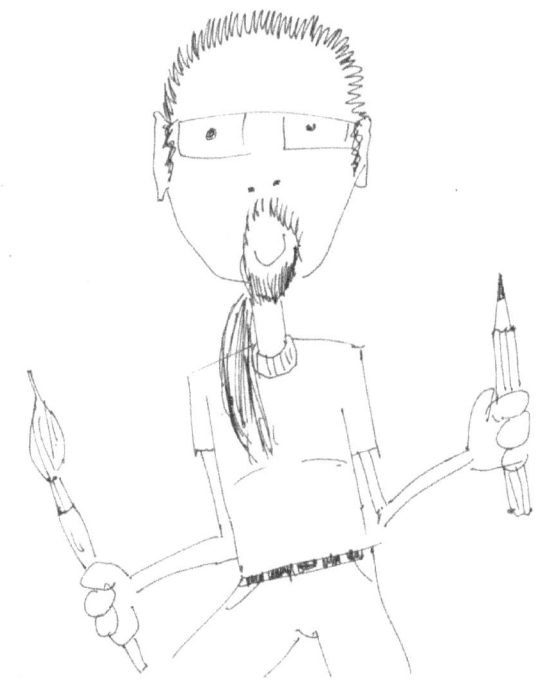

Moments later...X...

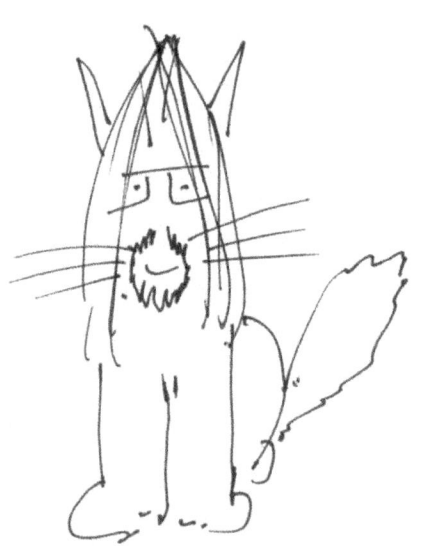

MEOW!...X...

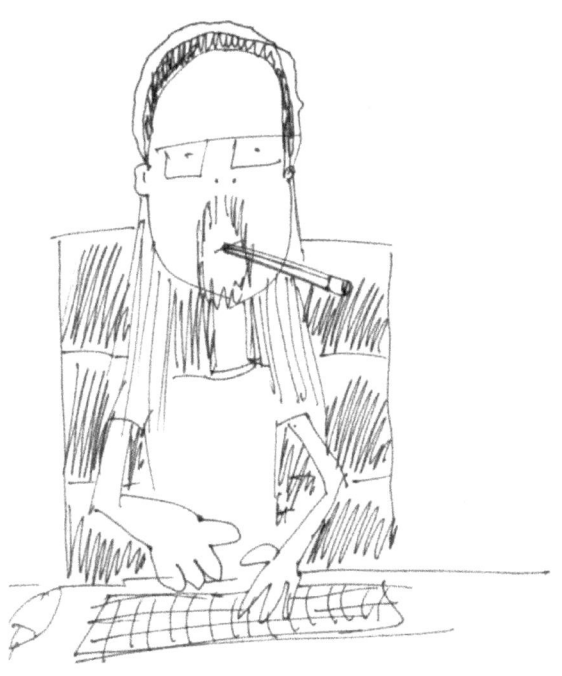

Must do some work a
while...X...

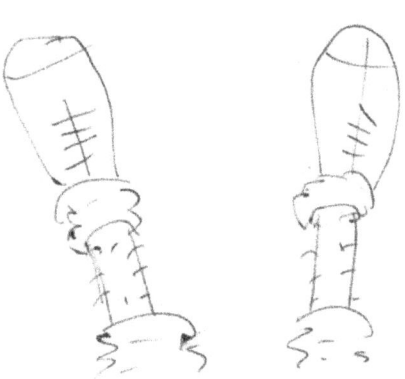

My chair moved...X...

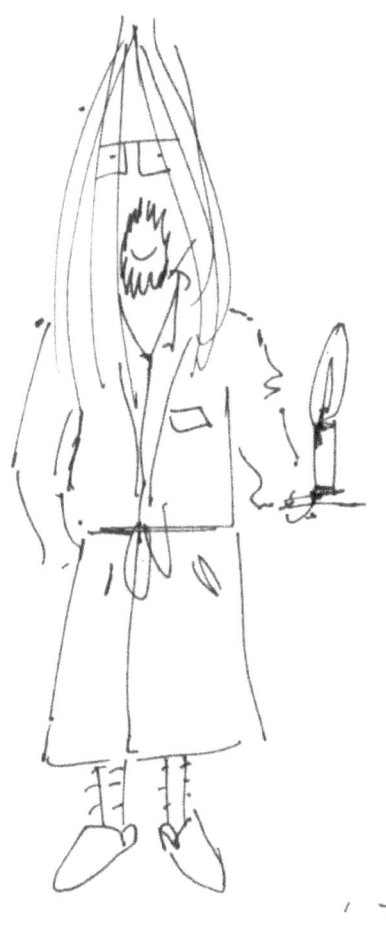

Nearly bed time...X...

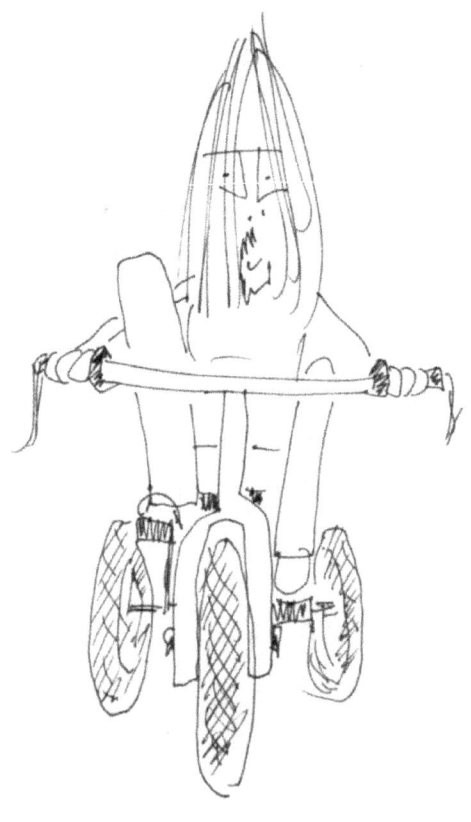

Easy rider...X...

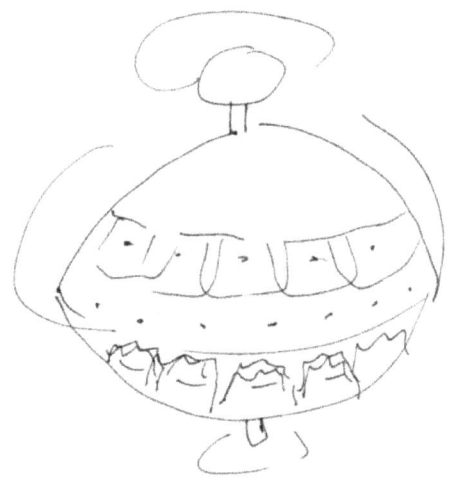

Oh bugger! I'm dizzy...X...

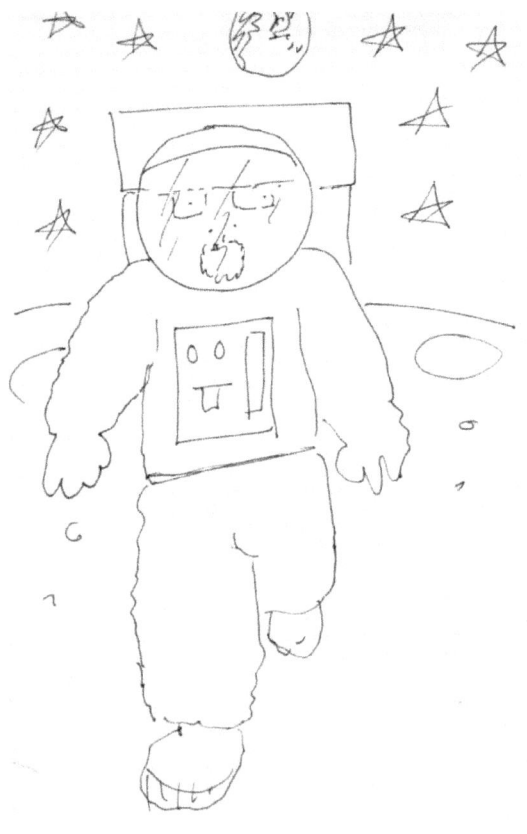

One small step...X...

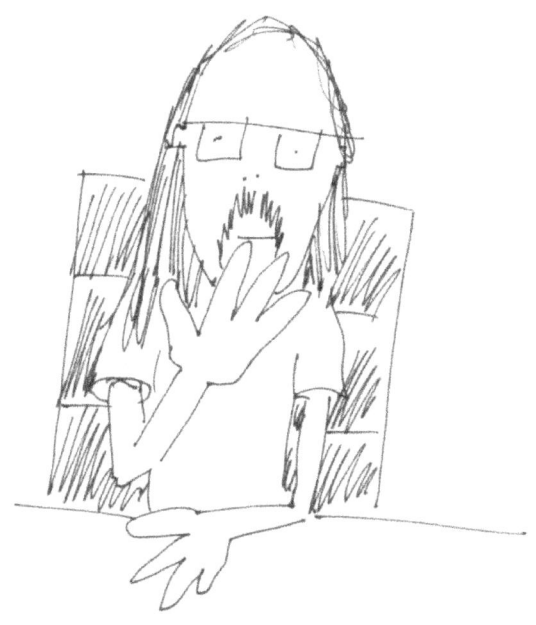

Pondering on the eve...X...

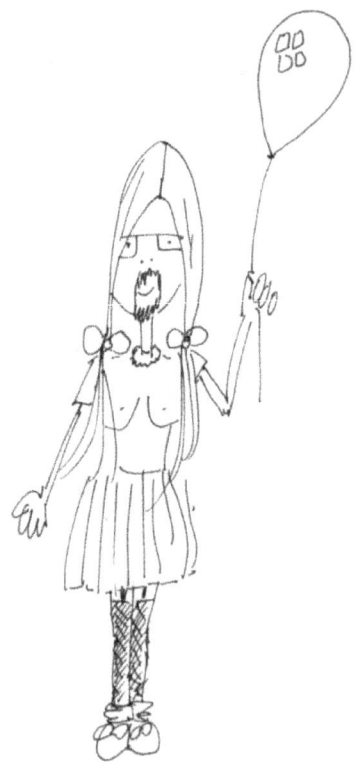

Rethinking my cosplay
costume...X...

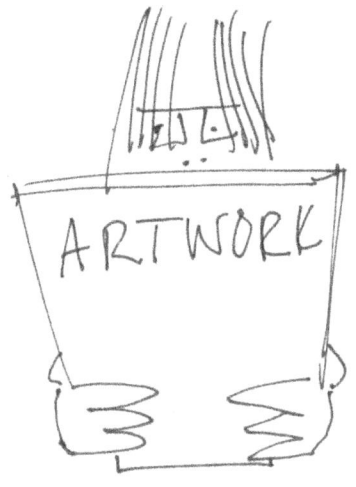

Steve brings my
artwork...X...

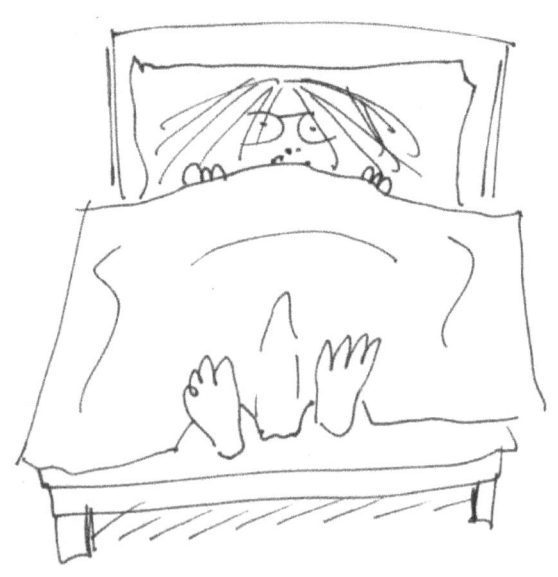

So soon...X...

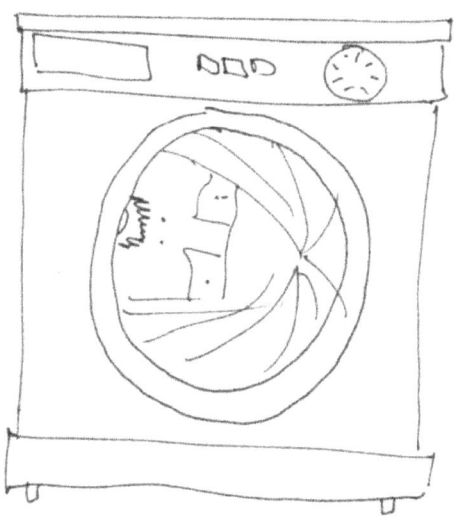

Something went wrong
washing towels...X...

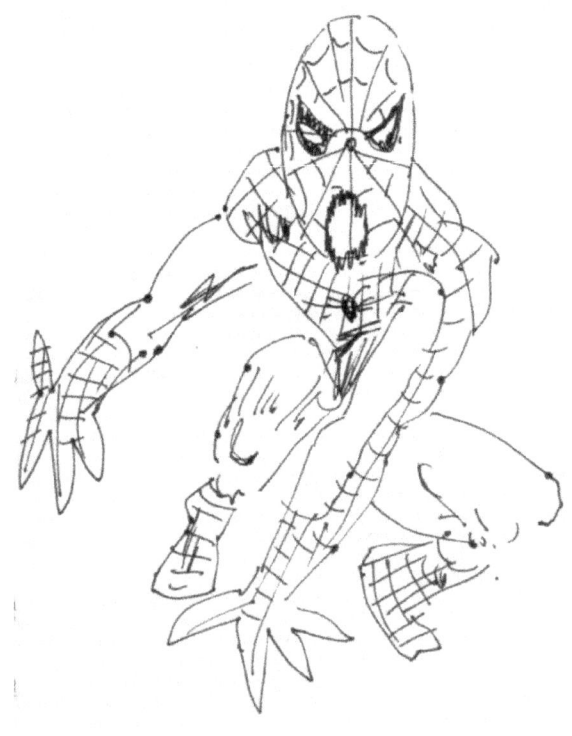

Spider-Mark...X...

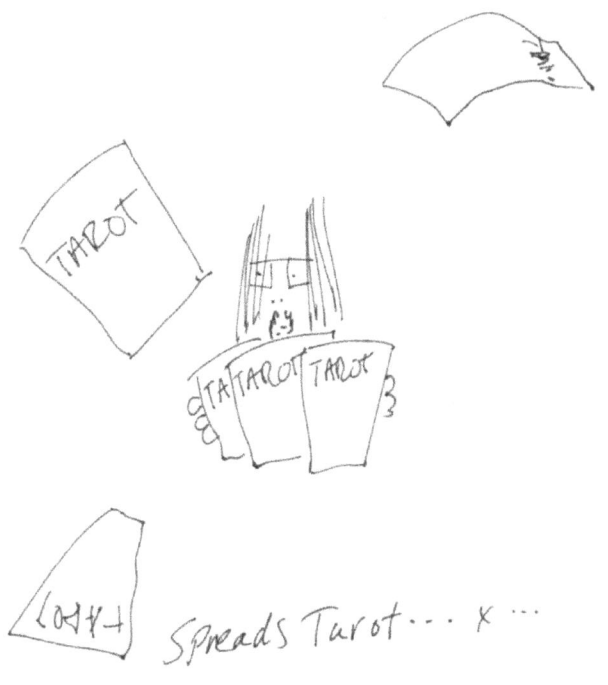

Spreads Tarot ... X ...

Mystic Mark – Tarot
spread...X...

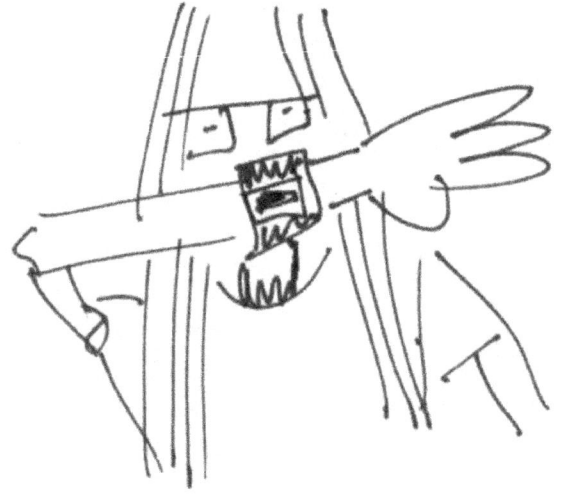

Still no Tom - checks
time...X...

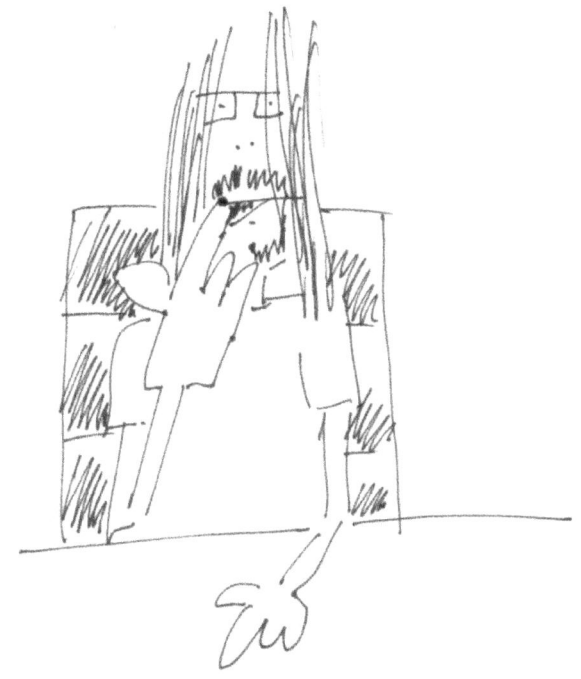

Still pondering the
eve...X...

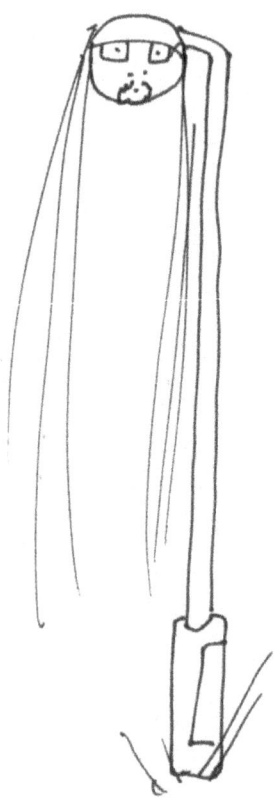

Mark the street light...X...

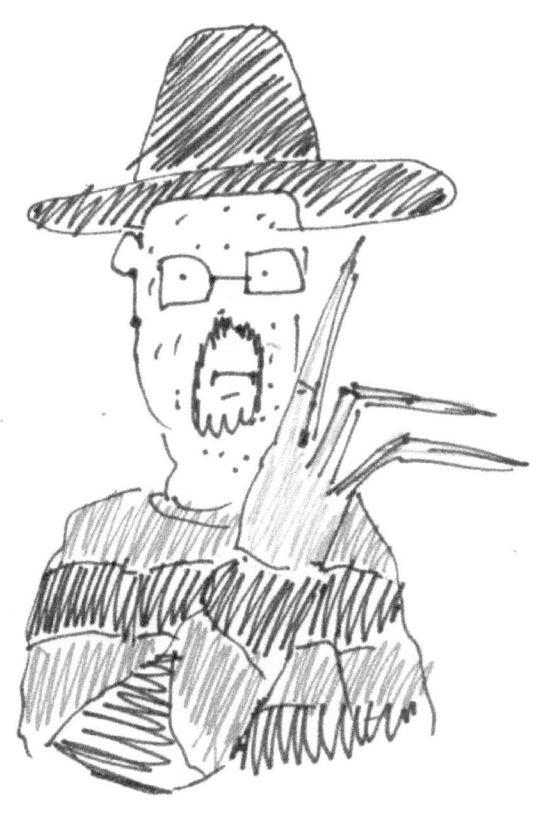

Sweet dreams...X...

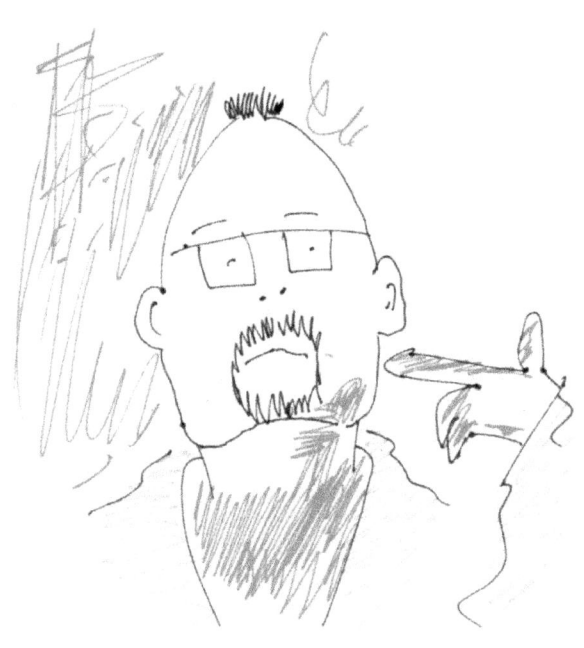

Taxi Driver...X...

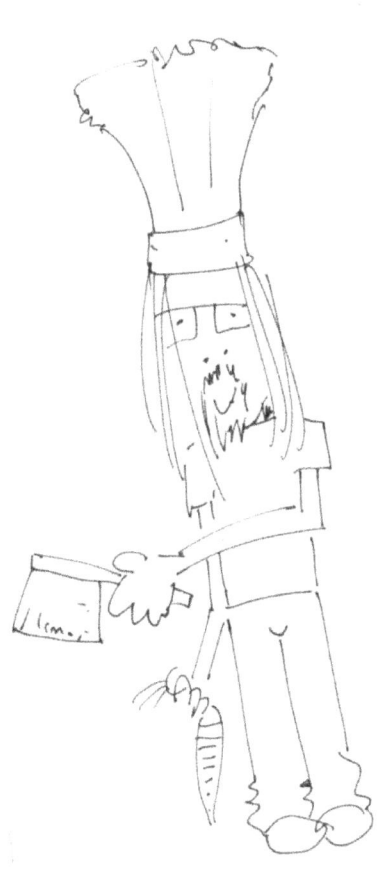

Tea time...X...

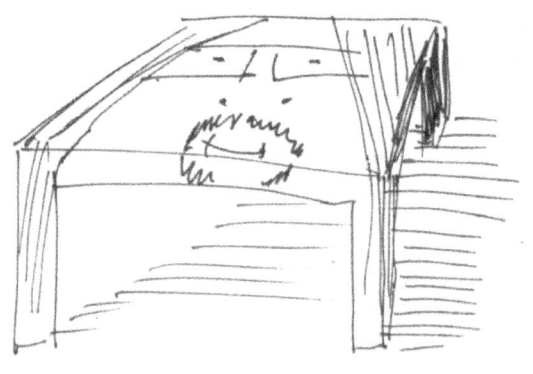

It was a mistake
teleporting while
carrying a table...X...

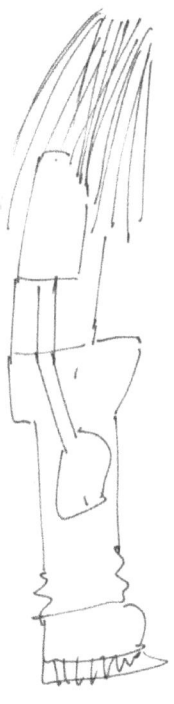

That was the Viagra not
the vit C. wasn't it?...X...

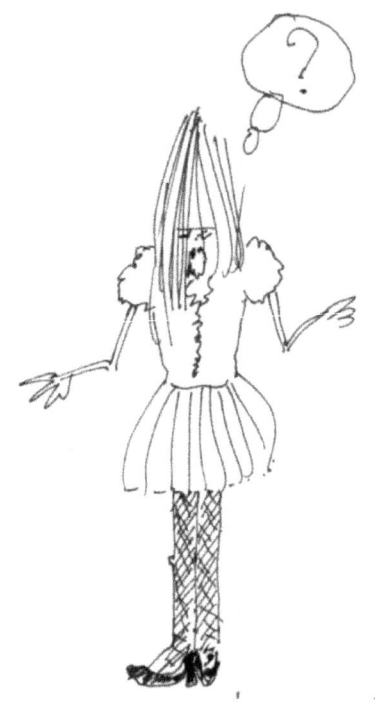

These really aren't my clothes, are they?...X...

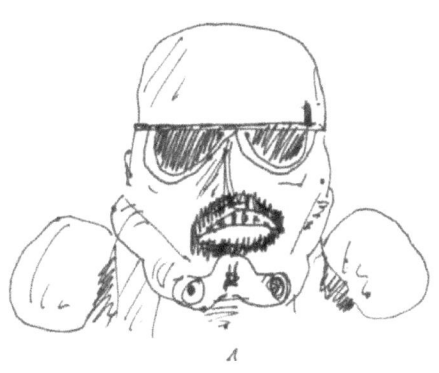

These aren't the droids
you're looking for...X...

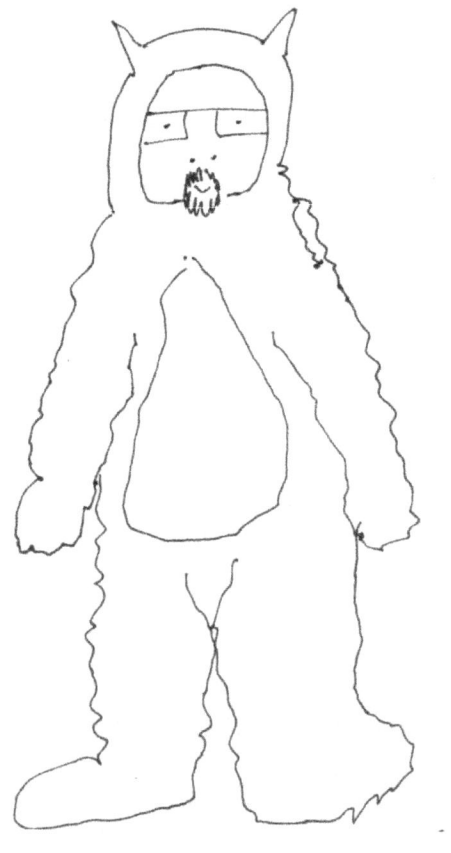

That's more like it...X...

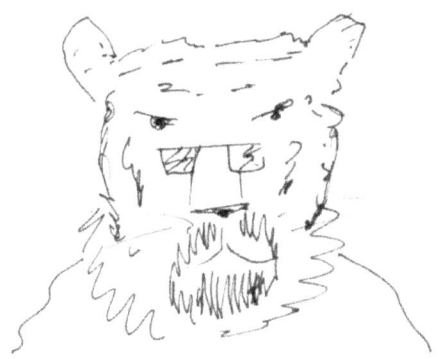

Grrrrr!...X...

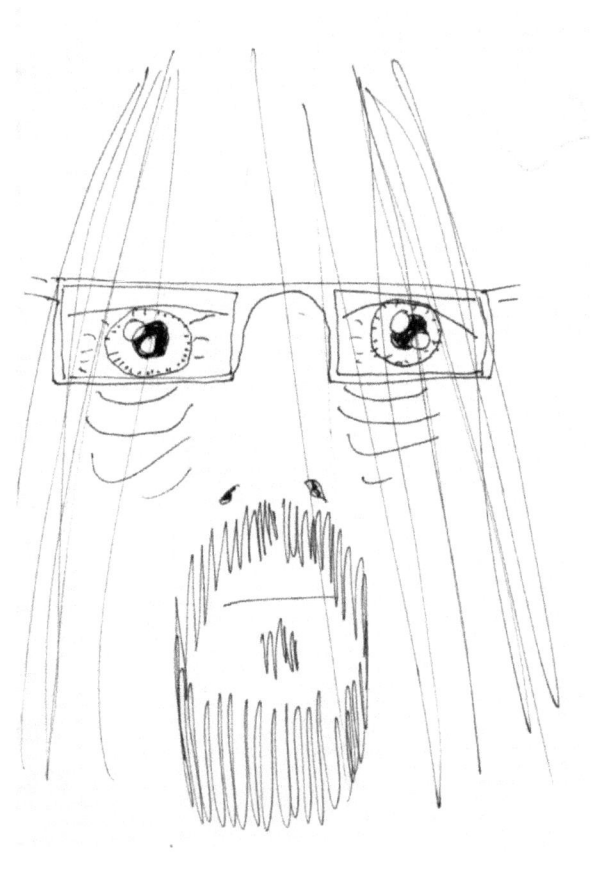

Tired...X...

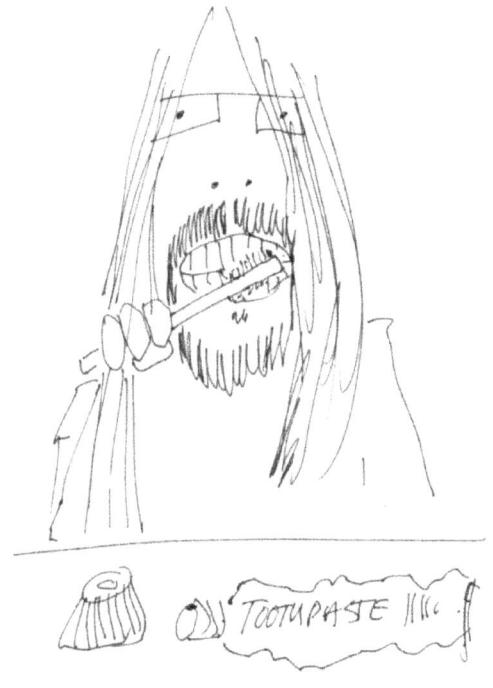

To do list...X...

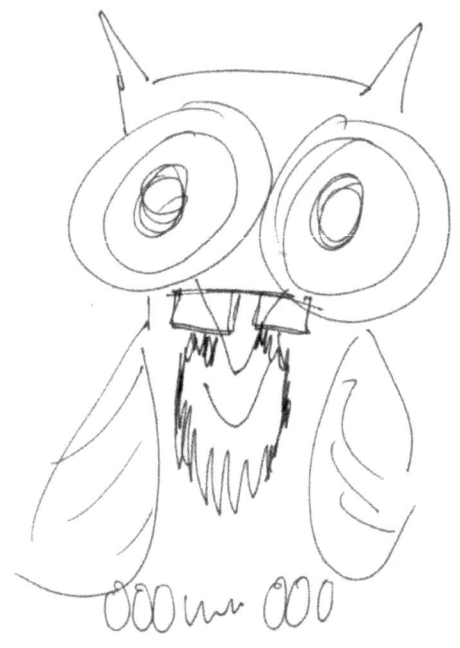

Twit!...X...

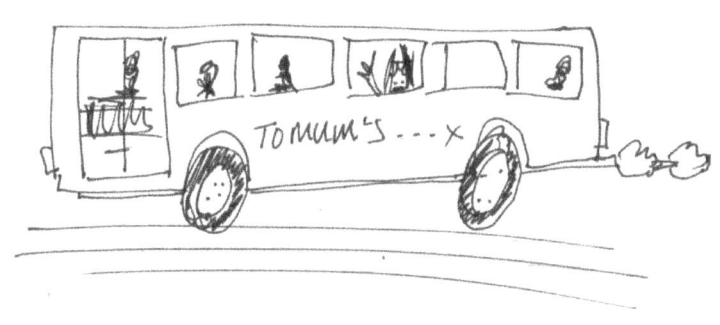

To mum's...X...

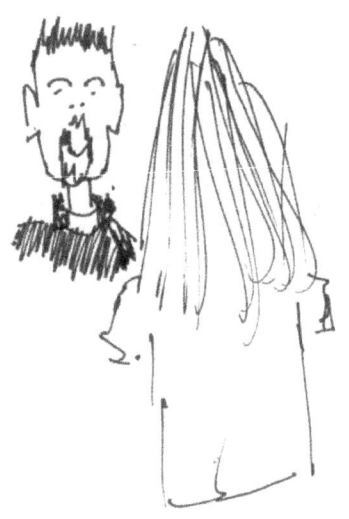

Tom came...X...

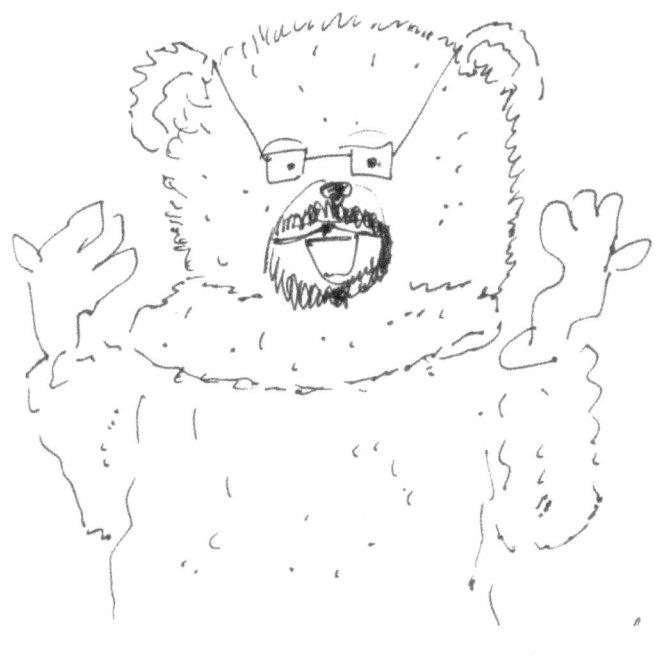

Up above the streets and
houses...X...

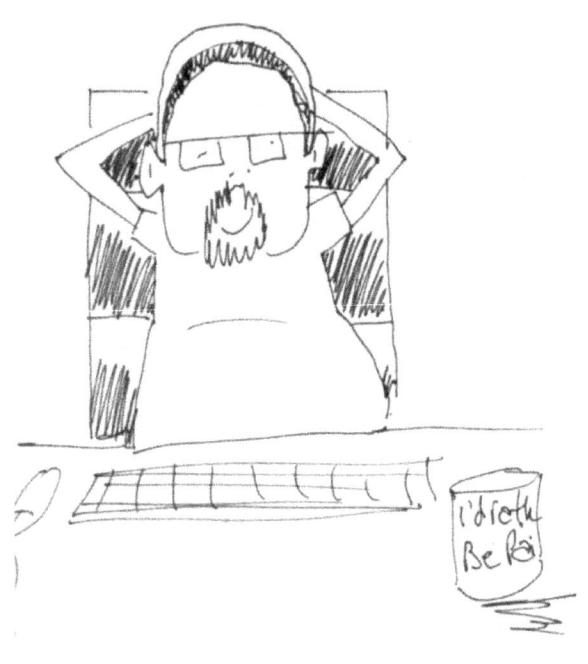

Up to date with the
editing, now coffee...X...

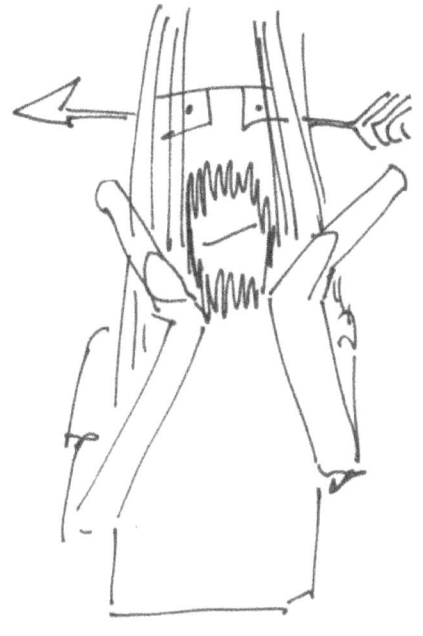

Thinking about lost love
- cupid got it wrong...X...

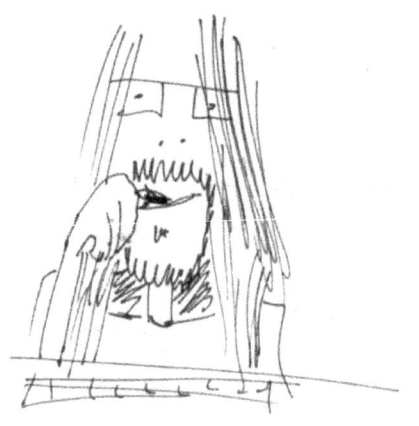

Watching Don
Hemmingway and having
a suck...X...

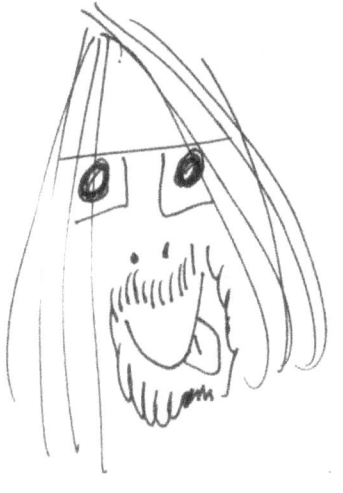

Watching Holly on This Morning...X...

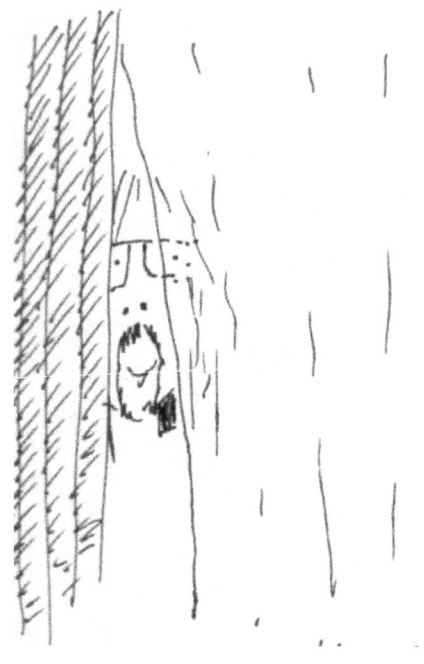

Why have there been
three police cars outside
all day?...X...

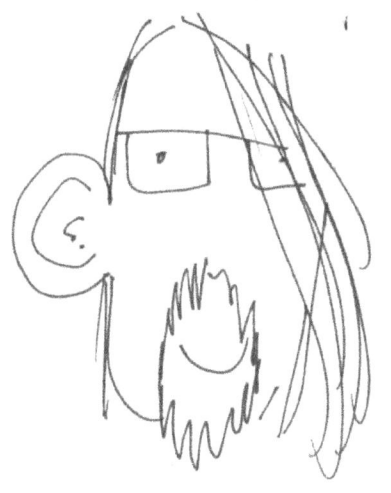

Waiting for the doorbell
to ring...X...

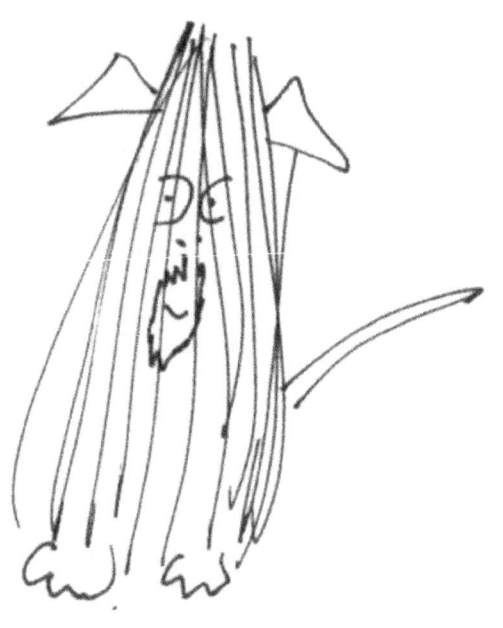

Wuff! Wuff!...X...

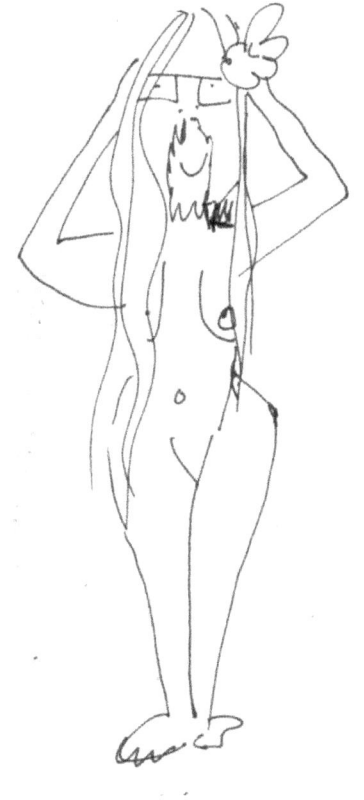

XXX...X....

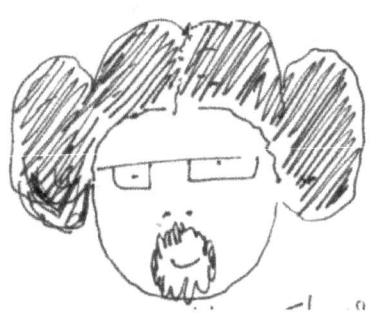

You're a little short for a
storm trooper...X...

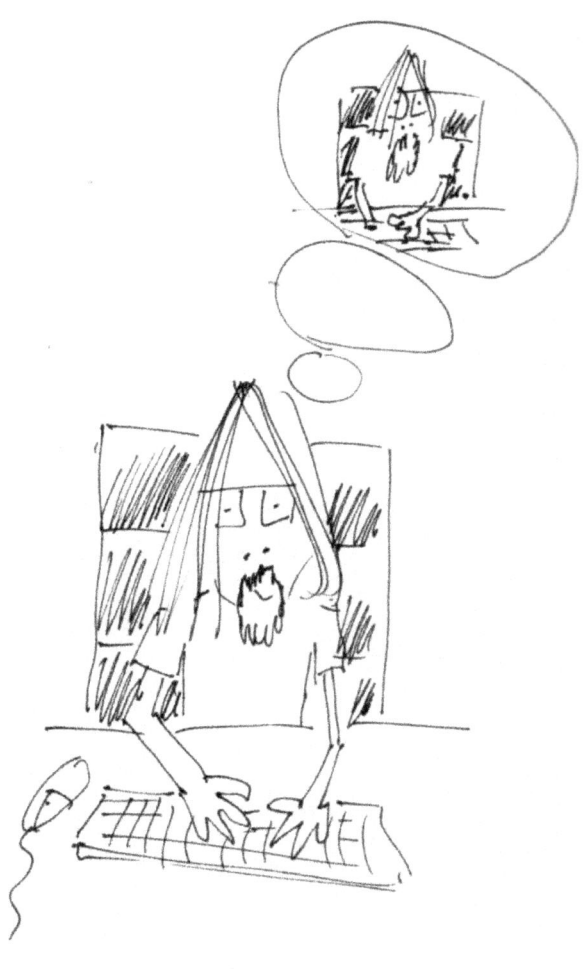

?...X...

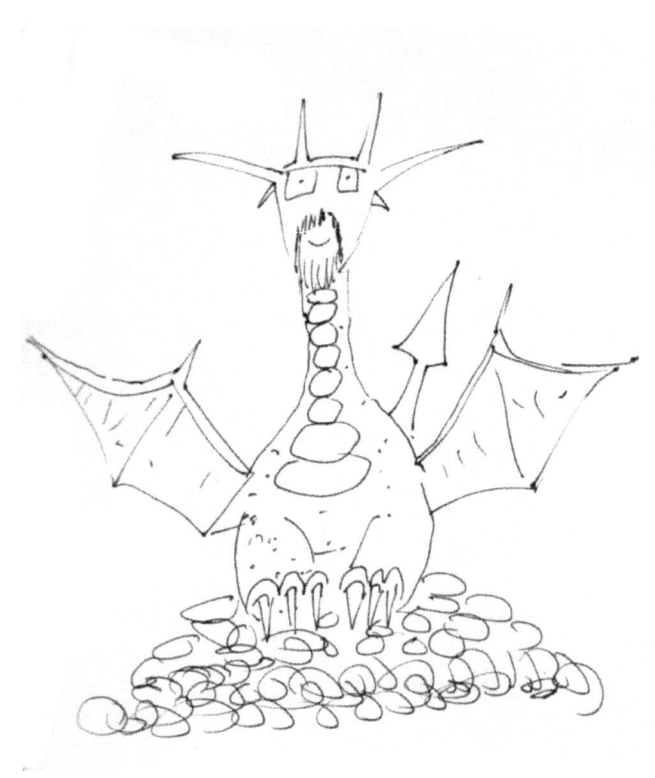

It's my gold!...X...

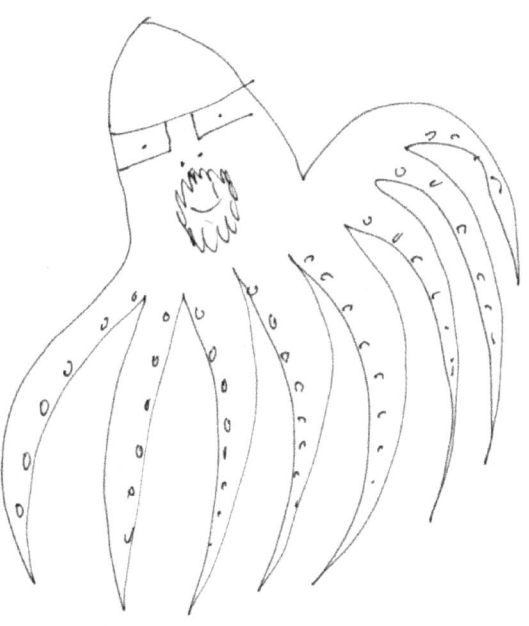

I can count to eight -
stuff you education!...X...

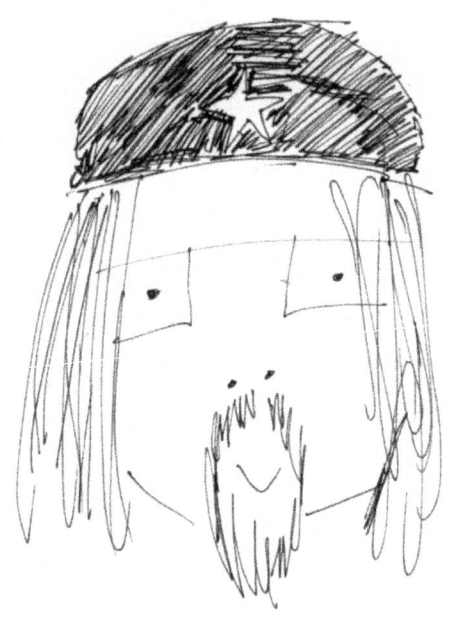

Viva la revolution, but
bring your own
cornflakes...X...

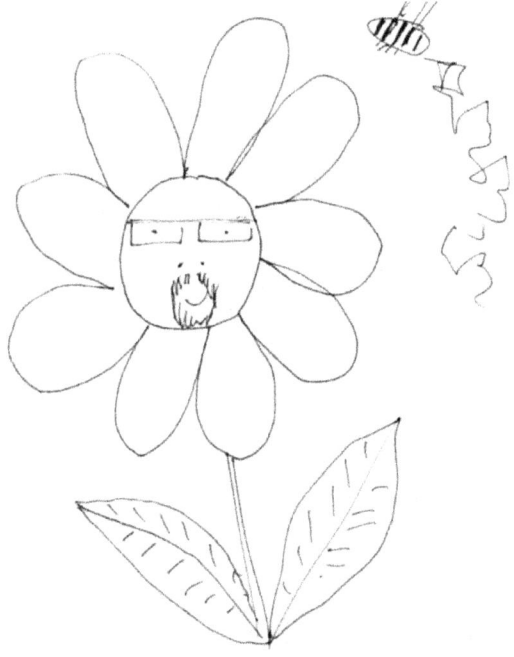

Flower Mark...X...

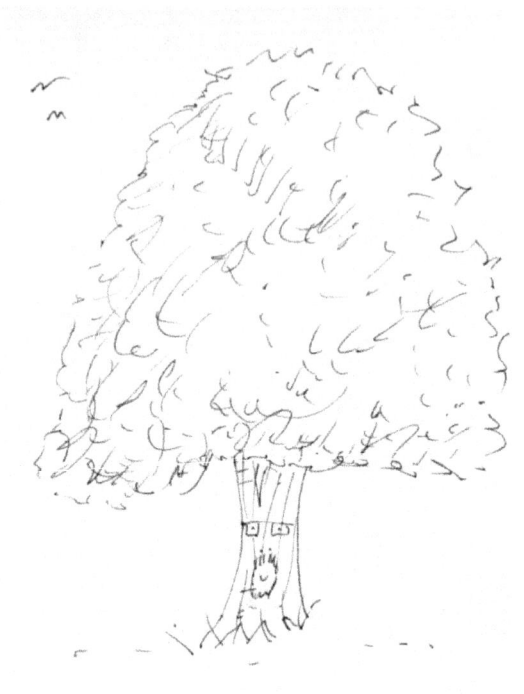

Mark the Mighty Oak –
there 'Ent' no use in
complaining...X...

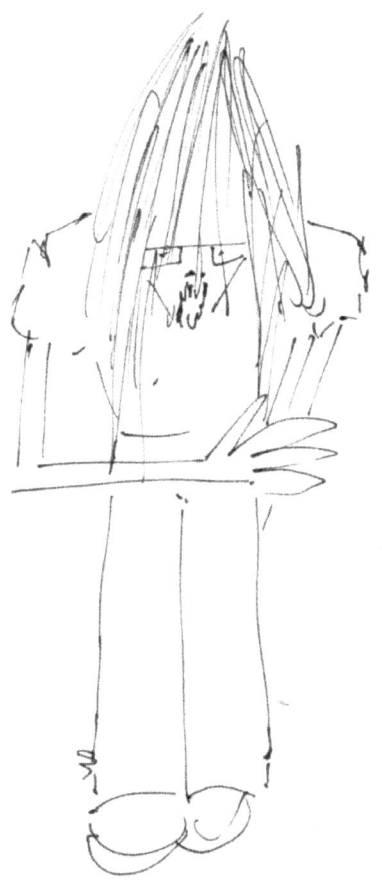

Thanks...X...

## Thanks

I'd like to thank everyone that found my selfies amusing, funny or just plain silly. They were lots of fun to do.

A very special thanks to Debbie Hill who proof read my book and to all those who sent me suggestions for selfies.

And many, many thanks to all those who bought my book. I hope you have enjoyed this spell of silliness.


Thanks,


Mark Pettifer...XX...

Other titles:

The Travellers' Rest

Pipe Fairies Revolution

Pipe Fairies II Secrets

All available on Amazon – print and Kindle – Pipe Fairies Revolution is also available on Kobo.

Come find me on Facebook and my public email is:
mpettifer63@gmail.com...X...